INSTEON
Smarthomes for Everyone

INSTEON: Smarthomes for Everyone
The Do-It-Yourself Home Automation Technology

iUniverse books may be ordered through booksellers or by contacting:

iUniverse
1663 Liberty Drive
Bloomington, IN 47403
www.iuniverse.com
1-800-Authors (1-800-288-4677)

ISBN: 978-1-4401-3343-5
ISBN: 978-1-4401-3344-2

Printed in the United States of America

iUniverse rev. date: 03/30/2009

iUniverse, Inc.
New York   Bloomington

For Jisty, Jathan, Jeanna, and Jira
Someday we'll meet in the Jamazon Jungle
--Jatt

Acknowledgements

I'd like to thank Steve Lee at SmartLabs, who has been an enthusiastic supporter of this book since I first emailed him with the idea of writing it. Al Choperena at SimpleHomeNet, Michel Kohanim of Universal Devices, and Harold Brooks at Interactive Electronic Systems have also generously supported this project with their time, expertise, and enthusiasm.

My most heartfelt thanks go to my wife and children. The time that I steal away for projects like these rightfully belongs to them. My wife makes my life so easy that it allows books like this to exist.

Introduction

My wife and I have friends who had built a home that included central lighting control, allowing them to light paths between rooms and "lighting scenes" for purposes such as watching a moving or cooking with the touch of a button. It was a pretty impressive system.

When it came time for my wife and I to rebuild, we knew we wanted to be able to do things like turn off all the lights throughout the house at bedtime and when we left the house, and light the way to the kids' rooms when we arrive home late at night and had to carry them in.

But when I looked into the cost, I was astonished. Our friends had spent over $35,000 to install their system, and our cost would be similar. I wasn't about to spend tens of thousands of dollars on a central lighting system—we didn't have that much room in the budget.

Centralized lighting systems require all lighting circuits to be run to a central location, and use a separate network of low-voltage wires run to specialized wall switches. The installation requires manufacturer-certified electricians, about twice as many labor hours, and the resulting system is difficult for the owners to program and reconfigure. Furthermore, when one of the central lighting controllers failed at our friends' home, it took down a few rooms for weeks until it could be ordered, shipped, and re-installed. Finally, while central lighting control systems can take commands from security systems and home theater systems, they can usually only be used to control lighting circuits.

I didn't like the idea of specialty wiring; there would be substantial extra cost in the increased lengths of cable, the low-voltage wiring for wall switches, and all the extra time and higher-priced labor it would take to install them. Furthermore, any "modern" electrical control system will be completely obsolete in 50 years, but your house will still be around. What if homes aren't wired that way when it comes time to retrofit the house? I definitely wanted a system that was wired the same way a typical home would be wired, to ensure compatibility with future systems.

So I started educating myself about home lighting systems, and discovered that new options had come to market since my experiments with X10 compatible de-centralized switches in the 1990s. Universal Power Bus (UPB), Z-Wave, INSTEON, and Zigbee all looked as though they might meet our requirements for a lot less money than a centralized lighting system.

The more I looked into it, the more obvious it became that INSTEON was the way to go. It helped a lot that INSTEON was the least expensive— about half as much as the other options. It also helped that INSTEON sold their devices directly online, and that from forum comments on various websites I could tell that regular people weren't having any significant trouble installing INSTEON devices and getting them working themselves. With rare exception, the forum conversations I read were very positive, and the few people that had reported problems were able to solve them quite simply.

So I bought a starter kit and setup a few devices in the house that we were renting while our new home was being built. I rewired a set of switches to create a 3-way switch that controlled both the living room and entry, and put all the lamps on the house on a central controller so we could turn off the common room lights. After living with INSTEON for a year, during which time the setup worked perfectly, we specified INSTEON for the new house.

INSTEON is so simple to use that even my small children have figured out how to program switches (which is actually something of a liability). It's quite clear that being able to leverage existing standards, labor practices, and installed wiring makes good economic sense.

Ultimately, our friends' system cost about $35,000 in hardware and labor, compared to $5000 in hardware and labor that it cost us to install a functionally superior system that controls a lot more than just lighting.

About this Book

This book is the product of my experience evaluating, buying, and installing INSTEON systems as both a "zero installation" retrofit in an existing home and as an integrated control system in a new construction home. It's the book I wish I could have bought when I started looking into INSTEON.

I've included my personal opinions and some discussion of how I've solved certain problems along with the general information about INSTEON, so I hope you'll forgive the "author's voice" that may be quite obvious throughout the book.

This book is a completely independent work that was not commissioned by SmartLabs, the company that developed and markets INSTEON. They have had no editorial control over the content, nor have I accepted any material support or evaluation devices from them. I did ask that they read through the book for technical errors prior to publication, and they have graciously provided some feedback in that regard. They have also provided stock photos of their devices. All errors, omissions, and opinions expressed in this book are solely my responsibility and should not be construed as being an official representation of any other party.

Universal Devices and IES, two independent third party manufacturers of INSTEON devices, have provided equipment for review in order to make this book more complete than my system alone would have provided for.

No matter what your level of INSTEON expertise is, this book is for you. The chapters of this book start with Smarthome basics and progress to a professional installation reference. More advanced users may want to skim through the first chapters until you reach the material that matches your level of expertise. You can help improve this book by sending any errors you find to: mstrebe@gmail.com

About the Author

Matthew Strebe is the author of seventeen books focused on the Windows operating system, computer and network security, and the business of computer services for publishers such as iUniverse, Sybex, Microsoft Press, and Wiley.

He is the founder and CTO of Connetic, an IT services corporation focused on managed services for the small and medium sized business market. He is also a founding partner and CTO of Zaxyz, A 3D-Printing technology research and development corporation that focuses on software development and materials research for inexpensive 3D object creation from digital sources.

His avocations include software development and electronics, and he enjoys sailing, motorcycling, automobiling, movies, and socializing. He lives in North County San Diego with his wife, three children, and a variable number of stick bugs, depending upon the season.

Chapter 1
What you can do with INSTEON

The term "smarthome" means different things to different people, but the core concept is easy to understand: A smarthome is a home where the major systems are computer-controlled to work in concert with one another and which can be adapted to the needs of the occupants.

> This chapter defines the role of INSTEON technology in the Smart Home. If you are already an INSTEON user, you may want to skip ahead to Chapter 2.

There are many different elements in a complete smarthome:

- **Lighting and Appliance control** to manage artificial lighting and appliances.
- **Environmental control** systems to manage natural lighting, ventilation, heating, air-conditioning, and irrigation.
- **Security and Access Control**, to save energy when the house is not occupied, and alert the owner to security, fire, or flooding events, and to enable remote monitoring of the home.
- **Entertainment Systems** to control home theater systems, computers, and ambient music.

This chapter will discuss the various components of a complete smarthome and the role of INSTEON in the smarthome.

TERMINOLOGY: NETWORKS AND HOME AUTOMATION

Bridge—A device that listens for signals on a network protocol and repeats or converts them for use on a different network using a different protocol.

Ethernet—The most popular protocol for connecting computers together to form a high-speed data network.

Home Automation Controller—A special purpose dedicated computer that comes pre-loaded with a home automation program to provide a single point of control of all home automation systems.

HVAC—Heating, Ventilation, and Air Conditioning (HVAC) systems manage the air temperature and humidity in a home.

I/O Controller—A device that sends input or output to a non-INSTEON device (such as a sprinkler valve, drapery closure motor, or siren) by opening or closing a circuit.

ISM Band—Free and unlicensed radio spectrum that device manufacturers can use without acquiring a specific FCC license to use the spectrum. There are three ISM Bands: 900Mhz, 2.4GHz, and 5.8GHz. Wireless INSTEON devices operate in the 900MHz ISM band.

Protocol—An agreed-upon method of communicating. In digital communications, a protocol defines how to address a message to a recipient, how to format the message in a way that the recipient will understand, and when to send messages in response to events.

Repeater—A device that receives and then re-transmits or regenerates a signal without modifying it. Repeaters are used to increase the distance that a digital signal can travel.

WiFi—"Wireless Fidelity" is wireless Ethernet data networking. Also referred to as 802.11a, b, g, or n depending on the speed and ISM band in which it operates.

Smarthome Technologies

No single technology or protocol is capable of managing all of the different systems of a Smarthome because fundamentally different signals are required for different circumstances. The technology required to report the status of a two-position switch is considerably lower-speed and lower-cost than the technology required to stream video in real-time.

It would not make economic sense to put the same expensive, high data-rate technology in the dozens of switches around your house as you'd put in a few cameras.

A smarthome will typically need at least two types of networks:

- A **Control Network** that is a low-speed, low cost network that manages large number of lighting and environmental controls. A control network is essentially a network that operates switches and other electronic controls of one sort or another.
- A **Data Network** that is a high-speed, high-cost network capable of moving large amounts of information between a small number of computing devices to enable Internet access, video streaming, and audio communication in the home. Your data network may be specific to a certain type of device, such as coaxial video cable for cameras and television distribution, or it may be a general-purpose digital network such as Ethernet.

This book focuses exclusively on the control network portion of the Smarthome—data networking is a very large topic and no single book could cover all the complexities and options available. Control network are considerably simpler and more easily solved. This chapter discusses data networks only to describe their role in the smarthome and to explain how the data network is interfaced with the control network.

To the degree possible, you should choose the two technologies you want to use for each of the two systems in the beginning and stick to them.

In your smart home, use a single technology for the control network, and another single technology for the data network.

You can also use compatible technologies that work seamlessly together for the two: for example, it's trivial to combine Ethernet and WiFi data networks because they were designed to work together, and it's trivial to combine X10 and INSTEON networks because INSTEON devices are compatible with both types of networks.

Using incompatible technologies, such as Z-Wave and INSTEON, will require a general-purpose computer or a Home Automation Controller to bridge the two technologies and will require substantial additional cost and configuration.

There are various options for connecting the control network and the data network together, ranging from a simple technology bridge to expensive and high functioning home automation controllers. If one network does not need to control the other, then you needn't bridge them together at all.

The Cable TV cabling and telephone cabling in your home will only play a peripheral role in your smarthome. Analog delivery systems such as coaxial cable and voice-grade telephone wiring are single-purpose; they can only perform the one function for which they were designed, and generally cannot participate in a data or control network without some sort of technology bridge. For example, I use a TiVo to "bridge" my Cable TV network onto my data network—the TiVo converts shows into data files that I can move around the house over my home network and watch whenever and wherever I want.

The data network choice has already been made for you: Ethernet and its wireless cousin WiFi dominate the data networking world, so there's no reason to choose anything else. Ethernet is built into anything that can participate on a data network these days, including digital video recorders, networkable security cameras, computers, and even cell phones. Both wired and wireless Ethernet have increased in speed over the years—from 10 to 100 and then to 1000 megabits per second for wired, and 11 to 54 to 110 for WiFi—and both standards have even higher speed options in development. The Ethernet vendors have done a good job with backward compatibility however, so you needn't worry much about the speed of individual devices on your network. With rare exception, everything will just work.

> HomePlug, an "Ethernet over powerline" solution delivers from 14Mbps to 200Mbps over home powerline wiring. The devices are about $100 each, and they are a very effective solution for creating a data network when Ethernet cabling or WiFi won't work. HomePlug and INSTEON do not interfere with one another and can coexist over the same powerlines.

The control network choice isn't so obvious: There are many competing technologies and they use many different methods to interoperate. This is similar to the situation in the late 1980s and early 1990s when numerous different data network choices existed. Ethernet at the time was considered "low cost, low capability" compared to its competitors Token Ring and FDDI—But its low price became a market advantage, allowing many more people to being using data networks than could afford competing technologies. All of the competing technologies worked, but the low cost and wide adaptability of Ethernet made its march to the top complete within just a few years. None of its rival technologies from fifteen years ago remain available for sale today.

INSTEON is well positioned to become the "Ethernet" of home control. It is the lowest cost among reliable options, it has more types of devices available, it is backward compatible with older X10 control network devices, it requires no special planning or equipment to use, and it has the largest market share amongst modern distributed home control technologies. It was exactly these attributes that allowed Ethernet to dominate data networking, and it's a safe bet that INSTEON will dominate home control.

Home Automation controllers, which are actually just special purpose computers, can be used to join together all the different home automation devices in your home to act in concert so that you can perform actions such as bringing down the lights when you turn on your television, or automatically begin recording video when a particular motion sensor activates. They do this by communicating using all of the various protocols you have in your home, allowing them to control devices on each different type of network.

With INSTEON, Home automation controllers are available, but not necessary. INSTEON-specific devices such as web interfaces, IR bridges, and I/O adapters can be used in place of home automation controllers to perform just about every function that a home automation controller can perform. I don't use home automation controllers in my installation because they are a central point of failure, are expensive, and they add an extra layer of complexity, but they do provide a central point of control for those willing to perform the required configuration.

What is INSTEON?

INSTEON devices are computer controlled power switches: Light switches, appliance switches, and specialty switches like dimmers and timer switches. Like the light switches you already have, INSTEON devices turn a light on when you press on, and off when you press off. They look like just like the light switches you have now.

But unlike traditional light switches, INSTEON switches can all talk to one another—they can tell other switches to turn off as well, or dim, or perform any sort of appliance control function such as drawing curtains or turning on a fan.

INSTEON devices can do this because every switch has a tiny computer called a microcontroller built in to it that communicates over your powerlines. Some INSTEON devices such as remotes and motion sensors communicate over radio frequency, and these signals are repeated on the powerline by INSTEON Wireless Access Points.

INSTEON creates a dual-mesh (radio-frequency and powerline) network of peer microcontrollers that all act as transmitters, receivers, and repeaters of all INSTEON signals. The signals are used to control the delivery of power to appliances. But this definition is like saying that a movie is a series of 1s and 0s on a plastic substrate compatible with the DVD format—it doesn't tell the story of what the technology can do.

INSTEON enables low-cost lighting and environmental control networks. It connects the various controls in your home (such as light switches, irrigation valves, vent fans, and appliances) together so that a person can use a single switch to control numerous devices simultaneously, or create time or event-based triggers to control devices.

INSTEON automates the control of home systems such as lighting and environmental controls and connects them to security systems, environment control, irrigation, entertainment, and other home control systems to enable a home to react to the needs of its occupants.

By creating a web of links between switches, homeowners are able to easily created complicated "scenes" that can bring up interior lighting automatically when a garage door opens, allow you to turn all the lights in the home off from your nightstand, or automatically turn off every light in the house at 1:00 a.m.

INSTEON devices are:
- Instantly responsive
- Easy to retrofit into existing homes
- Simple for the homeowner to configure
- Highly reliable
- Inexpensive
- Compatible with a vast array of devices

What INSTEON does on its own

A good way to define INSTEON is to explain what it can do. INSTEON is the control network component of a home automation system.

These are the functions that INSTEON alone enables:
- Multi-way light switching
- Path lighting
- Scene lighting

- Appliance control
- Environmental control
- Security

Multi-way light switching

Setting up multi-way switching is perhaps the simplest useful thing you can do with INSTEON. A multi-way switch is a set of switches that all control the same light. There is almost certainly at least one multi-way switch in your house right now—kitchen and living room lights usually are wired with switches at each of the entrances to the room.

Traditional multi-way switches have to be wired when the house is built or remodeled, because the wiring to the fixture must also go to each switch. Adding more switches to the control of the light makes the wiring more complex and the use of the light more complicated, to the point that wiring more than a 4-way switch is not feasible.

It is usually not cost effective to install a multi-way switch after a home has been built—the rewiring involved would take a considerable amount of time, you would have to open up walls and then patch them when the work was completed, and then re-paint. This would cost over $1000 for a typical home.

You can turn any switch in your house into a multi-way switch by replacing the switches with INSTEON enabled switches and linking them together. The only other requirement is that you also have an inexpensive phase coupler installed (which will be discussed later in this chapter).

For under $200 and using nothing but a screwdriver, you can setup reliable multi-way switching yourself. It would cost many hundreds to thousands of dollars to have an electrician rewire switches to enable multi-way switching for a light.

Path Lighting

Another common use for INSTEON is the creation of Path and scene lighting, which is similar to multi-way switching except that it turns on multiple lights along a path from a single switch, rather than controlling one light from multiple switches.

For example, you are used to walking in the front door and turning on the living room light. Then, on your way to the bedroom, you'd turn on the kitchen light, then the hall light, and finally your bedroom light. It's likely that your house would be wired so that most of those lights could be controlled at both entryways so you can shut them off as you move through the house. If not, you'd probably just leave them all on until bedtime when you'd walk around the house to make sure everything was off. This is how we've all lived our lives so far, and we're quite used to thinking in terms of controlling individual lights.

Contrast this with path lighting: When you walk in the door, you press the "Master Bedroom" path on an eight-button KeypadLinc keypad next to the door. The living room light, kitchen light, hall light, and bedroom lights all come up at once. Then, when you arrive in your bedroom, you press the "Path off" button on a similar controller by the door and all those lights (except the bedroom light) turn off at once.

> Path lighting requires that all devices along the path be switched using INSTEON switches.

Scene lighting

Scene lighting is the control of lighting in a room to establish a particular environment. Scene lighting is sometimes referred to as "mood lighting" or "ambient lighting." Think of Scene lighting as "path lighting with a theme."

For example, in your living room during the day you may want to have the shades open and no lights on. In the late afternoon, you may want to have the shades go down to block the low sun, and then at sunset you'd turn the overhead recessed lights on. Whenever you press the "TV On" button on your remote, you'll want the overhead lights to dim to 20% and all the shades to shut irrespective of the time of day. If it's overcast, you may want to have the interior lights on and the Windows open.

Scene lighting uses timers, events, and sensors to control the shades and lighting in your home to enable exactly these sorts of scenarios.

Scene lighting allows you to use the environmental controls that you probably just ignore now, such as drapes, shades, thermostats, and gas fireplaces, to automatically operate themselves during the day to establish the mood and environment you want to have around you.

Scene lighting requires all the devices involved—lighting, shade controllers, and the home theater system in this example, to be INSTEON enabled. To enable true scene control in a particular room, you would need to have all of your lighting and devices in that room controlled by the INSTEON control network.

Appliance control

INSTEON doesn't just control lights; any appliance that can be on/off controlled by plugging it in or unplugging it can be controlled by an INSTEON relay. This simple level of universal control is appropriate for devices like Home theater equipment, electronically controlled gas fireplaces, fans, and so forth.

For example, you could automatically turn off a fireplace when you turn on the television, turn lamps off simultaneously with light fixtures, or shut off window fans when the sun sets. Or you could turn off all you're "sleeping" home appliances at night when there's no chance than anyone would use them, reducing their power draw even further.

Environmental Control

INSTEON devices called Input/Output (or I/O) controllers are used to manage low-voltage devices and to detect the condition of switches and sensors such as window and door closures, leak detectors, motion sensors, etc. They can control low power devices such as shade rollers, window operators, sprinkler valves, and Heating, Ventilation, and Air Conditioning (HVAC) dampers.

I/O controllers allow you to set the condition of an INSTEON switch based on the value of a sensor. For example, you could turn on the lights in the living room and master bedroom if a window sensor detects that a window has been opened in a child's room—thus alerting you to the event. Or you could turn on patio lighting when a motion-sensing camera detects movement outside, thus automatically turning on path lights when you arrive home.

Security

Security systems are essentially large, integrated I/O controllers—they connect sensors to inputs, process the sensor inputs to determine when a security event is happening, and trigger outputs to ring alerts or alarms.

INSTEON I/O controllers can be use to create simple security systems that turn on lights or alarms in response to events like windows or doors being opened or a motion sensor being triggered. Creating the sophistication of an actual alarm system is possible, although it would likely be less expensive to simply use an existing alarm system and integrate it with your INSTEON system.

Integrated INSTEON

INSTEON does plenty on its own, but a complete smarthome security system will need to integrate the INSTEON control network with a high-speed data or video network. Fortunately, INSTEON supports a complete range of home control software and various technology bridges that can connect these systems together.

Sophisticated security systems

Using a stand-alone security system allows you to define more complex events than INSTEON alone would provide. In addition to operating as a stand-alone security system, INSTEON compatible security systems include an INSTEON bridge so that the security system can control INSTEON devices and listen for INSTEON events. For example, you can configure an INSTEON enabled alarm system to automatically shut off all the INSTEON controlled lights in your house when you arm the panel for exit, and bring up certain lights when you come back into the house.

As of the time of this writing, the Elk M1 Gold alarm system is the first INSTEON enabled alarm system available. The Elk alarm panel can send INSTEON codes when any of its sensors, such as motion sensors or door and window open sensors are triggered. This allows you to use any security sensor device as an INSTEON controller.

While the Elk M1 Gold is specifically adapted for INSTEON compatibility and can directly control INSTEON devices, you can integrate any security panel with INSTEON by connecting the security panel's alarm outputs to an INSTEON Input/Output Controller's inputs. This allows you trigger INSTEON events from any security alarm event, and it doesn't require specialty software or hardware to do it. You can also do the reverse—connecting Alarm panel inputs to INSTEON I/O outputs to trigger alarms.

Remote home control

There are a number of ways to remotely control an INSTEON smarthome. Most of computer software applications that are compatible with INSTEON can create a website that will allow you to log over the Internet to access and control INSTEON Devices. Most dedicated home automation controllers also serve a web site for remote control via the Internet.

INSTEON specific devices, such as the SmartLinc, the SimpleHomeNet EZSrve or the Universal Devices ISY-99i are designed to provide a web interface for INSTEON control at a very low cost—between $100 and $400 dollars.

Be especially careful about allowing remote access to your home control systems. Connecting anything to the Internet makes it potentially hackable and can create a security risk—especially if you're not completely familiar with the various security protocols and techniques that are necessary to secure the device. Even if you are good with computers, you didn't write the application software installed in the automation controller and you can't guarantee that it was written with proper attention to security in mind.

Sophisticated Scene management

Sophisticated scene management refers to a system that responds to what the occupant of the home is doing, rather than what the occupant has asked for, in order to control the home automation. Sophisticated scene management uses multiple sensors and inputs going to a home automation controller which interprets those inputs in order to detect the presence of occupants and enable various lighting and environment scenes.

Sophisticated scene and environment management is considered by many to be the "nirvana" of smarthome control. However, it requires a considerable amount of forethought about what you want and a considerable amount of programming, testing, and de-bugging.

Most people who deploy the equipment for sophisticated scene management never actually do the work required to get it working—irrespective of which technology they use. There are a number of reasons for this, but primary amongst them is the fact that it's nearly impossible to determine all the ways in which the system might be incorrectly triggered—for example, using motion sensors to detect when someone has entered the home theater and using that input to turn on the television is going to annoy someone who is only there to vacuum the carpet, or who is carrying a sleeping child. No system can really determine the intent of a person, and so any case that is uncommon will create unwanted reactions from the system.

For that reason, I recommend designing to specific, real-world uses such as "I want these seven lights to come on when I press one of these three switches" rather than vague ideas like "I want the system to detect when I've left the house and turn off everything"—because that statement doesn't define what specific, measurable events constitute "leaving," and the system may not know that another person remains in the house (who will be surprised when everything goes dark).

By simply defining a switch by your front door as "Exit" and "Arrive," you can use your human ability to know what's appropriate and simply assert to the home control system what it should be doing. This is vastly simpler than trying to deploy enough sensors to manage every possible case.

The amount of testing and troubleshooting involved in developing a properly functioning scene management system is considerable and ongoing. If you expect a third-part smarthome integrator to understand your requirements and program the system perfectly in advance of using it, you will be disappointed when they inevitably fail.

With sophisticated scene management, you'll have to do the testing and debugging yourself through much iteration as you discover the capabilities of the system and your own needs. Start simple, and grow into it as you become comfortable with the technology. Chapter 4 covers designing scenes in detail.

What you cannot do with INSTEON

INSTEON provides only the control network portion of a home automation system—it does not provide the data-networking portion. For that reason, there are components of home automation that INSTEON alone cannot provide.

Home Theater

INSTEON is minor component of a home theater. Dimming the lights before a movie comes on, drawing the shades, and perhaps shutting down home theater components at night, are the ways in which INSTEON supports a home theater system. I use an INSTEON ApplianceLinc to power on the fans that cool my A/V cabinet when I power on my television.

Video surveillance

INSTEON doesn't have the bandwidth required to move video through a house—this would have to be done over a high-speed network or coaxial video cable.

INSTEON support the multimedia portion of a smarthome by transmitting and responding to "triggers"—indications that there is something has happened that other devices need to respond to. For example, in response to an INSTEON motion detector, door or window sensor, or a light being turned on, you could trigger the I/O inputs on a Pan/Tilt/Zoom (PTZ) camera to focus on the area where the even occurred—automatically. This ensures that you automatically get video coverage of the things that are actually occurring in your house. Most surveillance network cameras have I/O inputs that can be configured to move the camera to pre-specified locations when they're tripped, and INSTEON I/O controllers can trigger those inputs.

Audio & Intercom

There is not enough bandwidth available over the powerline INSTEON network to move audio throughout a home. Therefore, it cannot be used to transport audio data for such purposes as Intercoms, baby monitors, or ambient music.

It is possible to create an INSTEON-RF Intercom system because there is enough data available to transmit voice over the INSTEON-RF network. No devices exist to do this at the time of this writing, however.

Technologies that are not compatible with INSTEON

Because INSTEON works over the power lines and in the 900 MHz ISM radio-frequency band, there are a few relatively obscure technologies that it is not compatible with.

> Plan the use of the ISM bands to avoid interference. In my home, INSTEON operates in the 900MHz ISM band, WiFi Networking in the 2.4GHz band, and the cordless phone operates in the 5.8GHz ISM band.

You may have some interference with 900MHz telephones, baby monitors, or other 900MHz ISM band equipment, although the interference would be minor and intermittent. In practice, I haven't had any significant problems with this, but interference is always a possibility with RF devices. Buy equipment that operates in the 2.4GHz or 5.8GHz ISM band instead.

Problems with INSTEON

No technology is perfect for all purposes; Engineers always make trade-offs to enable the features they want at the price-point that the market wants, and INSTEON is no exception. All of INSTEON's competitors are designed with different constraints, and the consequences of those constraints determine which technology will work best in a particular environment.

The address space is limited

This is a problem that won't affect you, but will limit the future growth of INSTEON and necessitate a follow-on protocol that may not be completely compatible with current devices.

INSTEON device addresses are 24-bits long, which provides 16 million unique addresses. This length was chosen as a trade-off between a large enough address space to uniquely identify a vast number of devices and yet small enough to be transmitted rapidly on the wire.

16 million sounds like a lot, but when you consider that the average home will have at least sixteen devices, INSTEON will run out of address space before one million home installations. There are 100 million homes in the U.S., and about one billion worldwide. The address limitation problem for INSTEON is not remote enough if the protocol becomes extremely popular.

There are no easy choices when the limit is reached:
- SmartLabs cannot simply start re-using addresses because that will cause unlikely but random failures when someone buys two devices with the same address.
- There is no simple way to address the devices manually or randomly in an installation, and requiring an address to be applied to devices

after purchase will cause an "enrollment" process that makes installation more difficult to use.

- SmartLabs also cannot simply increase the size of the address space and remain compatible with older devices. There are hacks they could try to implement such adding extra address info as data, but that would not be compatible with existing devices.
- While firmware updates for existing devices could take them to 32 bits and solve the problem, asking people to update the firmware of every switch in their house is not reasonable.

If INSTEON becomes popular enough that SmartLabs begins running out of address space, they will almost certainly come out with "INSTEON 2" series that have a 32-bit address space allowing for four billion devices. These devices would be incompatible with original INSTEON devices out of the box, but will probably be software reconfigurable to work on a 24-bit INSTEON installation with a manually assigned address.

In any case, the problem is years into the future in the worst case, and certainly not a problem for early adopters.

The Internet has the same problem: It's 32-bit IP address space is not enough to address all the computers in the world already, and "hacks" such as network address translation have been developed to conserve addresses. Some countries will run out of Internet address space in the next few years, forcing the move to a new 64-bit version of the Internet Protocol.

Simultaneous Switch Presses

Two INSTEON switches cannot begin transmitting at exactly the same time. This is because only one INSTEON signal can travel over your electrical wiring at one time.

In practice, this is so unlikely to occur accidentally that it is almost not worth mentioning: Two people would have to tap a switch within about fifty milliseconds of one another in order for the problem to express. I calculate the odds of that occurring in a home with five occupants to be about one in ten thousand switch presses—or perhaps once per year. However, if you tap two paddle switches with two fingers at the same time, you'll see the problem: The two INSTEON signals "step on" one another and the command is garbled so nothing happens. If you're even slightly off of the exact same time, the second device will wait for the first one to finish and then transmit its signal, so you'll notice a delay for the second signal.

> The odds of simultaneous switch pressing go up with the number of occupants of the building—not with its size. INSTEON installations can be any size, but should be limited to buildings with fewer than 60 occupants to keep collisions unlikely.

Retry Delay

Every once in a while you'll notice a light take a moment longer than you're used to turn on, especially if you're turning on a large group of lights. This is a case where the light missed the original group on command, and came on later during the acknowledgement phase when the original sender decided that it did not receive an acknowledgement from the light and re-transmitted the command to turn on. This isn't actually a problem; it's the feature that makes INSTEON networks so much more reliable than X10 device networks, because in an X10 network, the light never comes on at all if the original command is missed.

Incorrect Cross-linking

Some INSTEON devices that are setup to control other lights, such as KeypadLincs, do not get status reports of the light if the light has been controlled by another switch and all the devices are not cross-linked correctly. Unfortunately, incorrect cross-linking is common.

For example, if you turn a light on with a KeypadLinc, the KeypadLinc will light the button to indicate that the button is on. But if you turn the light off with a switch that is not linked to the KeypadLinc, the button will remain lit even when the light is off. When you press the lit KeypadLinc button, the light will go out to match the status of the light, and the next time you press it the light will go on, as you would expect.

It's not a significant problem and in most cases it is easy to fix, but you should be aware that switch status lights won't always accurately tell you whether a remotely controlled light is on or not.

The locally controlled load is special

When you have a group of lights linked together and you press one of the switches, the locally controlled light (the light actually wired to the switch you pressed) will come on instantly while the linked lights will come on a fraction of a second, but noticeably, later. This occurs because there is a slight amount of time required to send the command to the other lights, but locally controlled lights come on instantly.

INSTEON switches always control their local load—you cannot setup a switch to control other devices without controlling it's own local load. This is rarely a problem, but it is something to be aware of.

LEDs can be too bright

Most INSTEON switches contain relatively bright LEDs (usually white) that make convenient night-lights for most rooms. They can produce too much light for bedrooms at night if they are close to a sleeper, however. Consider ICON line switches, which have a dimmer amber LED, for bedrooms instead of INSTEON SwitchLinc lights, or use KeypadLinc switches, the current version of which can be programmed to turn off their local LEDs completely.

Power consumption

Each INSTEON device will consume between 5 and 10 watts continuously based on the measurements I've made with my power meter, whether the circuit it controls is on or off. This is a trivial amount of power individually—far less than a night-light.

But I have fifty INSTEON devices installed in my home. This means that INSTEON devices consume about 300 watts at all times—the equivalent of leaving a television on continuously. At 0.3KW/h * 14¢ per KW/h in my area, INSTEON costs me 4.2¢ per hour to operate. With 720 hours per month, that's $30 additional on my power bill for a yearly operational cost of $360. Not quite so trivial in those terms. Your mileage will vary.

That's pretty much it for problems. There's a very slim chance that sometime in the lifetime of your INSTEON network that you'll hit a switch and nothing will happen because somebody else in the house hit a switch at the exact same time. This hasn't happened to me except when I did it on purpose.

Not compatible with Modified Sine wave inverters

Modified sine wave inverters are used to convert DC from cars and photovoltaic solar power systems inexpensively. These inverters create A/C using switching electronics rather than through the radial motion of a generator, so the signal they produce is not a smooth sine wave; it is a square wave or modified sine wave.

INSTEON devices are not compatible with square wave or modified sine wave power inverters, and will quite likely be damaged by them. The one device I tested on the output of a modified sine-wave inverter never worked again after having been connected to it.

> If you have a photovoltaic solar system installed in your home, or if you intend to use your plug-in electric hybrid vehicle or R/V as an emergency power generator for your home, this warning applies to you.

If you have a photovoltaic system or if you intend to use an automobile or R/V as an emergency power generator for your home, you will have to use a true sine wave inverter in order to be compatible with INSTEON devices, which will cost considerably more than a modified sine wave inverter.

Summary

To create a smarthome, you need a control network. Distributed control networks such as INSTEON are the least expensive reliable way to create multi-way switching, path and scene lighting, and to control appliances throughout your home. While INSTEON cannot perform the functions of a high-speed data network, it can integrate with your data network to provide the complete smarthome experience.

Chapter 2
Understanding Home Electrical Wiring

Understanding home electrical wiring is important to understanding how and why INSTEON works the way that it does. It's so fundamental to how INSTEON works that it's important to cover the basics before we get too much further into the book.

> This chapter concentrates on electrical theory and home electrical wiring in general. Chapter 6 focuses on wiring specifically for INSTEON home automation. If you already know how home electrical wiring works, feel free to skip to Chapter 3.

After a short digression concerning electrical safety, this chapter will focus on home electrical power theory and practice, including how power phases work, how switches and outlets are wired, and the differences between early electrical wiring and modern electrical wiring.

This chapter contains a lot of potentially confusing terminology, and many of these terms mean slightly different things in different contexts. If you're not very familiar with electrical terminology, be sure to refer back to this terminology section as you read if you don't know how a particular term is being used.

TERMINOLOGY: ELECTRICAL HOME WIRING

110VAC—110 Volts AC. Derived from one half of 220VAC supplied to the home, supply voltage is actually 120VAC that typically drops to 110VAC at the device, so supplies are typically referred to as 120VAC and devices are referred to as 110VAC. Both numbers are used interchangeably and they mean "residential lighting and outlet power."

220VAC—220 Volts, Alternating Current. The type and potential voltage of electrical current delivered to homes in North America. The actual voltage varies from 240 to 220—240 is delivered to the house, and the voltage generally drops to 220 under load, so power supply is typically referred to as 240, while device draw is typically referred to as 220. They're used interchangeably to mean "Residential home supply power."

Amp—A unit of electrical quantity. In the "water analogy," amperage would refer to the amount of water flowing past a particular point. Volts x Amps = Power, which is measured in Watts.

Circuit breaker—A switch designed to shut off if current exceeding its rating is drawn through it. Circuit breakers on 110VAC circuits are rated for either 15 or 20 amps, and on 220VAC circuits for either 30 or 50 amps in North America.

Circuit—(1) Any complete path between two different electrical potentials through which electrical current can flow. (2) A path of lights and/or outlets in a home controlled by a circuit breaker.

Earth—The same thing as Ground. Earth is more typically used in the UK.

Gang—An amount of space taken in a junction box by a single switch or typical dual outlet. A "single gang" junction box has space for one switch; a "double gang" has space for two, etc.

Gauge—Also referred to by the acronym AWG (American Wire Gauge standard) is the thickness of the conductors in electrical wiring. 12 or 14 gauge wire is typically used for 110-volt circuits. The lower the gauge, the more current the wire can deliver without overheating.

Ground—A conductor leading to actual earth ground. Ground is usually a bare copper wire or may be insulated green.

Fixture—an installed lighting receptacle that is wired to power and (usually) a switch. Light bulbs are installed in lighting fixtures.

Hot—The energized wire of a circuit that has electrical "potential" when connected to neutral (or, by accident, ground). Also frequently referred to as "Live" or "Line." Hot may be black, red, or orange wire according to the National Electric Code (NEC) that most localities adopt as their electrical code.

Junction Box—A metal or plastic box set into a wall for the purpose of fixing switches our outlets in place. Electrical wiring is run from circuit breakers to junction boxes, and from junction boxes to load devices. In situations where a junction box cannot be used, a metal ring or surface-mount box may be used.

Kilowatt Hours—the unit of power consumption used to measure home usage at your meter and on your bill. If you run ten 100-watt light bulbs for one hour, you have consumed 1 KW/h of electricity. An occupied home will typically consume between 1 and 3 Kilowatts per hour.

Line—The wire on a switch that is connected to "Hot."

Load—(1) any device that consumes power, (2) The wire on a switch that should be connected to the device to be energized. Load is connected to line and power flows through the switch to the load device when the switch is in the on position but not when the switch is in the off position.

Low-Voltage wiring—Low voltage wiring is used in systems that operate below 50 volts, and which are therefore not considered deadly, and so are not regulated by electrical code. Low-voltage wiring is used for data networking, video and telephone wiring, doorbells, fire alarms, and security systems. Unlicensed contractors can legally install low-voltage wiring in most localities.

National Electric Code (NEC)—A private organization that develops best practices and standards for home and commercial power wiring. The vast majority of municipalities adopt the NEC standards with little or no changes, so the NEC standards are what all-electrical appliances and devices are manufactured to comply with.

Neutral—The center voltage between the two hot phases of 220VAC power supplied to a home. Neutral is connected to Earth ground at the electrical main point of entry (MPOE) in most houses. Current flows from the Hot wire through the energized device, to neutral. Neutral wires are white or less commonly grey in color.

Phase—In residential home wiring, phase refers to the two legs of 220VAC power, which are split into two 110VAC legs by splitting their voltage with a neutral wire that is at the center point of voltage between the two hot conductors.

Romex—standard two-conductor, three-conductor, or four-conductor

PVC shielded electrical home powerline cable.

Switch—A device that interrupts an electrical circuit, causing work to stop.

Switch-Leg—A switch that is wired from the device that it powers rather than from a hot circuit. Switch-legs use typical black and white-romex wires to run from the device to the switch, with the black wire connected to the load and the white wire connected to Hot at the device.

Traveler—The cable leading from one switch to another in a three-way switch circuit.

Volt—A unit of electrical potential force. In the "water analogy," voltage would be analogous to the pressure or speed of the water flowing through a full pipe. Volts x Amps = Power, which is measured in Watts.

Watt—A unit of measure for total electrical power. A watt is 1 amp of electrical power at 1 volt of potential for 1 second of time. A typical home circuit can deliver 110 volts x 15 amps or 1650 watts of power to a device.

Wirenut—A threaded conical cap that can be twisted over two or more bare wires to permanently but reversibly join them together. Wirenuts are the standard method for wiring switches and outlets to electrical cables in junction boxes.

Electrical Safety

Electrical safety is paramount when working on home electrical wiring. 110 and 220 volt power is deadly, and should be approached with extreme caution.

> Much of this section may seem obvious to some readers, but remember that this book is written for a wide audience of people, many of whom may have never worked on electrical circuits before.

Most municipalities allow homeowners to perform their own wiring. Some cities require that a certified electrician perform all electrical wiring. Check with local codes to ensure that it is legal for you to perform your own electrical wiring before proceeding.

Hire a qualified electrician

If you have any reservations about your skill in working with electrical circuits, hire a qualified electrician to install wired-in INSTEON devices. If you will be performing the design of your system and the programming of your INSTEON devices, any qualified electrician can install them. There's nothing special about wiring for INSTEON, so the electrician needn't know anything about INSTEON other than that he will need to wire the neutrals to the switches, which is not necessary with traditional switches.

Never work on an energized circuit

Never work on an energized circuit. Shut off circuits at the circuit breaker panel before opening a junction box faceplate or removing a fixture.

If you live with other people who may not realize you're working on electrical circuits, place a danger tag on the circuit breaker switches you have shut off indicating that they should not be turned back on until you remove the tag.

Besides just being good safety sense, breaking circuits is required because INSTEON devices are powered by the neutral line and can be damaged by the "arcing and sparking" caused by attempting to wire them up in an energized circuit. Causing a short while you are attempting to wire an INSTEON device is also highly likely to damage the INSTEON device.

Use AC voltage detectors or multimeters

AC voltage detectors and multimeters allow you to probe individual wires in a junction box for the presence of AC current before you work with them. Even if you think that you've shut off the correct circuit, multi-gang junction boxes frequently contain wires run on different circuits. You may have correctly powered off the circuit for the switch you intend to work on, only to be shocked by another cable in the junction box.

Always use an AC voltage detector or a multimeter to check for power on every wire in the junction box before you work and after you've shut off the circuit breakers. You can purchase an AC voltage detector or multimeter at any home improvement store or Radio Shack for about $25.

Never work in the house alone

Do not work on electrical circuits in the house alone. If something should happen that renders you unconscious, you will need someone else to administer first aid and potentially call 911.

Never leave a junction box open at the end of the day

You may be tempted to leave junction boxes open with wires exposed at the end of a long day so you can pick up where you left off the next morning. It's unlikely that you'll be able to control what other occupants in the house may do, however, and they will likely want to re-energize circuits that you're working on. If you have to leave an installation incomplete, cap off all bare wires with wirenuts and plate over the junction box so that it is safe to re-energize the circuit. You'll also need to put a wirenut over any wires left bare when an installation is complete.

Use the right tools for the job

It is especially critical that you use the correct size wirenuts for the gauge of wire and the number of wires when you install anything in a junction box. Wirenuts that are too tight or too loose may work their way loose when you're stuffing them back into a junction box. Always twist wires together before applying a wirenut.

> While Scotchlok brand wirenuts do not require pre-twisting, it is often difficult to tell what brand of wirenut you have in an existing home.

INSTEON has done a good job of making INSTEON devices thin enough to install in the space taken by a traditional switch, but they do occupy more space than a typical switch leaving less room for wires. Most junction boxes will be a tight fit, making correctly sized wirenuts all the more important. Buy a large selection to make sure you've got the right wirenut every time.

Get a low-voltage (such as 3.6v), low-speed, low torque electric screwdriver with a swappable battery if you are installing a large number of INSTEON devices. Screwing and unscrewing dozens of long junction box screws will wear you out quickly if you're doing it manually. Avoid using a drill however—they are generally too powerful and will strip junction box and faceplate screws.

Use a gauged wire stripper of the correct size to strip wires. Don't use your teeth, a pair of scissors, or a utility knife, as these methods are needlessly unsafe.

> Any home improvement store or Radio Shack will carry all the tools you need to perform electrical home wiring safely. A complete set of tools will cost less than $50. I like to keep all my electrical tools in a tool belt to keep them handy (and to let my spouse know that I'm doing something useful).

Understanding Electricity

Understanding electricity is fundamental to understanding electrical home wiring, and how lights, switches, and circuits work. This section explains electricity and basic electrical terms.

Electricity

Electrons orbit the nucleus of all atoms in much the same way that planets orbit the sun (except that electrons orbit in a sphere, not just in a flat plane). If an electron is pulled away from an atom by some force, then the atom has a "hole" and becomes strongly attractive to other electrons until the missing electron is replaced. If an atom has too many electrons orbiting it, it will shed them when it comes near an atom that that can more readily accept the electron.

Skip to the next section if you already understand the theory of electricity.

Electricity is the potential to do work that exists when electrons that are able to move freely between the atoms that make up an electrically conducting material such as a metal wire are put under an electromotive force such as magnetism. The interaction between magnetism and electricity is called electromagnetism.

Materials (such as metals) that allow electrons to flow freely are called conductors, whereas materials that strongly resist the flow of electrons (such as plastics) are called insulators. Insulators do not easily give up or accept electrons, whereas conductors swap them freely. Conductance is the measure of how freely a material conducts electrons, and resistance is the measure of how much a material insulates against conductance.

In a conductive material (a conductor), electrons will move freely from atoms that have too many electrons to atoms that have too few. The atoms that need electrons will pull them from their neighbors, who immediately replace them by pulling them from their neighbors, in an instant chain reaction reaching back to the atoms that have a surplus. The flow of electrons from atoms with a surplus to atoms with a scarcity is called electricity.

Electricity explains how batteries work: The positive (+) side of the battery contains chemicals that need electrons, and the (-) side of the battery contains chemicals that have a surplus of electrons (electrons have a negative charge). When you plug the battery into a circuit, a path is created between the positive and negative reservoirs, and electrons flow through the circuit causing work to be performed. Positive and negative electrical potential are referred to as positive or negative polarity.

Resistance converts electricity to light and heat. This is how electric heaters and incandescent light bulbs work: Running electricity through a moderately resistive conductor causes it to heat up and produce both heat and light. Optimizing for heat makes an electric heater, choosing materials that optimize for light creates a light bulb.

All devices that cause electricity to perform work, such as light bulbs, vacuum cleaners, coffee makers, and televisions, are called "loads" and they all resist the flow of electricity by some significant amount. A resistor is a load that performs no work other than to heat up and resist the flow of electricity. Resistors are used to ensure that electrical power cannot overwhelm a load that cannot itself resist the flow of electricity sufficiently for its own safe operation.

All conductors have a slight amount of resistance, so they all heat up slightly as electricity moves through them. The larger a conductor is, the more electricity it can safely carry. The more electricity the conductor carries, the warmer the conductor will get.

Electricity will always take the shortest, most conductive circuit (path). If you have a battery with two lights connected in parallel between positive and negative, the light with the lower resistance will glow brightest, and the light with the higher resistance will glow very little if at all. A short-circuit is caused when electricity is able to take a "short cut" rather than flowing through the intended load such as a light bulb. Short-circuits are very dangerous because they provide very little resistance to the flow of electricity, allowing the electricity to heat up conductors and destroy electrical devices.

Magnetism and Electricity

Magnetic fields cause electrons to flow in materials even when no imbalance naturally exists because the movement of the magnetic field "pushes" the electrons in much the same way that a pump pushes water.

Moving a magnet past a conductor causes electrons to flow in the conductor, and this effect can be used to reliably generate electricity. Generators work by using some mechanical force to turn a coil of wires inside a magnetic field, which creates electrical potential at the ends of the wire coil. This effect converts mechanical force, such as that generated by a gas motor or a wind turbine, into electromotive force called electricity.

Generating Electricity

Generators can be made to generate positive polarity (a scarcity of negatively charged electrons) at one end of the wire and negative polarity (a surplus of negatively electrons) at the other. This is called a Direct Current generator.

The "speed" (motive force) of the flow of the electricity is measured as voltage, while the "area" of the flow is measured as amperage. Multiplying "speed" time "area" provides total quantity of power, which is measured in watts. 10 volts times 10 amps = 100 watts of electrical power. You can think of this in terms of water at your tap: The speed of flow times the area of the pipe cross-section = total quantity of water.

Generators can also be made to reverse electrical polarity once each turn of the generator so that electricity moves back and forth through the wire, with each end of the coil swinging from positive to negative and back in opposite "phase." This is called Alternating Current and generators that create AC are called alternators.

If you imagine water flowing between two reservoirs on a moving seesaw through a pipe that connects them, you'll understand how one end is positive (full) when the other is negative (empty), and how the electrical force (measured as voltage) flows back and for the between them. The two sides are said to be in opposite phase with one another. When the seesaw is level, the two sides are equal, and at that moment, there is no electromotive potential between them until one side goes lower. That middle point when the current reverses direction is 0v (zero volts).

A switch is an electrical valve that interrupts an electrical circuit by disconnecting the conducting wires. With conductivity interrupted, no power can flow and work stops. This is exactly like turning a faucet on and off—the valve interrupts the flow of water.

Power stations use alternators that create AC power with tremendous electrical force, which is then transmitted through the powerlines, which create a circuit connecting every building in the power grid. The buildings tap off the electrical force and reduce it through transformers to a level (generally) safe for humans to work and live around. This is similar to municipal water supply—large diameter pipes feed smaller pipes, all the way to your home where small pipes deliver the water to individual faucets.

In your home, electrical service comes into a main electrical panel, where it is connected to a number of special switches called circuit breakers.

A circuit breaker is a switch that has a heavy spring that causes it to push back against being switched on. To turn it on, you push past the force of the spring until the switch clicks into place, which holds the circuit on.

Power flows through the switch via a special type of conductor that will deform if it gets too hot. When the conductor passes too much electricity, its natural resistance will cause it to deform, which releases the clip that holds the switch, which shuts off the circuit. If too much electricity is drawn through the circuit, the circuit breaker will heat up and break the circuit, interrupting the flow of power and preventing a dangerous discharge of electricity.

> Circuit breakers prevent the wires built into your home from overheating when an appliance or device short-circuits, or when you make a mistake while wiring.

Each circuit breaker controls the delivery of power to a circuit of installed fixture lighting or outlets in your home. Generally, four to ten fixtures or outlets will be wired to a single circuit breaker, usually delineated by room so that the circuit breaker can be conveniently labeled. Outlets and fixtures should not be combined on a single circuit, but exceptions to this rule are common. Shutting off a circuit breaker makes it safe to work on the de-energized circuit.

Finally, power to a fixture is interrupted a final time by the light switch. A single light switch will control power to one light or a group of lights all having the same function, such as a chandelier, counter lights, or a pair of sconces in a room.

Understanding Alternating Current

Alternating Current power, or AC, is electrical current that rapidly cycles from positive to negative and then back again in a short time period. AC current is used for power transmission because it does not suffer from increasing loss over long distances due to resistance the way that Direct Current (DC) does. The period of the alternating current (referred to as Hertz or Hz) is 60Hz in North America so that electric clocks can be made to tick one jiffy once each cycle (A jiffy is 1/60th of a second). In much of the rest of the world, 50Hz is used.

Phases

AC power in the United States is delivered to homes as single-phase alternating current on two hot conductors at 220-240 volts with a center neutral, hereafter referred to as simply 220VAC.

At the circuit breaker, the neutral, which is at the mid-point of potential between 0 and 220, is wired to earth ground, and the two hot conductors are split into two 110VAC legs. This is somewhat erroneously referred to as "two-phase" power (which is actually something else entirely), but in residential electrical wiring when people refer to two phase power, they mean single-phase 220VAC residential power split into two legs.

This book follows the common convention of referring to each 110VAC leg as a phase.

Each phase feeds half of the lighting and accessory outlets in the home, with outlets for high voltage devices such as dryers and stoves fed by both.

240-220VAC

Devices that require 220VAC power, such as electrical dryers and stoves, use both phases and a large round outlet. 220VAC outlets are directly wired to a single circuit breaker rated for either 30 or 50 amps.

120-110VAC

Most home electrical appliances and lighting are designed to operate on 110 volts in North America. Electrical circuits in the home are generally attached to either 15 amp circuits for typical use, or 20 amp circuits for particularly high-draw circuits or areas of the house where more power is required from outlets, such as the Kitchen. The rating of a circuit is defined by the thickness or gauge of wire used in the circuit and the rating of the circuit breaker at the panel. 12-gauge wire is required for 20 amp circuits; 14-gauge wire can be used for 15 amp circuits.

Calculating power usage

Calculating how much power a device will draw is easy: Just multiply its rated amp or milliamp draw by 120 (the maximum voltage delivered) to get its power usage in watts. 1000 milliwatts = 1 watt.

To determine how much draw there will be for a particular circuit, sum the power draws of all the devices on the circuit. When you don't know what the draw of the appliances will be, the typical average used is 200 watts per outlet, for up to eight outlets on a single 15-amp circuit. This includes the presumption that not all outlets will be used.

```
15 amps x 110 volts = 1650 watts / 200 watts per device = 8 outlets
```

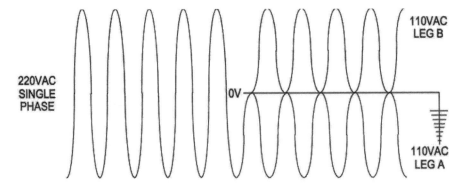

Figure 2.1: 220VAC split into two 110VAC legs

AC Wiring

Power coming into the home at the main point of entry is divided into a number of circuits at an electrical panel. The electrical panel will have a circuit breaker for each 220VAC outlet and a breaker for each circuit of 110VAC lighting fixtures and appliance outlets. A typical 110VAC circuit will connect four to eight lighting fixtures or outlets depending on the expected draw.

220VAC outlets typically have two hot wires and a neutral. They may also have a ground.

Hot

Also sometimes referred to as "phase," "line," or "live," Hot is the lead in an electrical cable that carries the electrical potential compared to Neutral. When a device is connected to both Hot and Neutral, a circuit (or path) is formed, and current can flow through the device (devices are also called a load). Power flowing allows the device to operate.

On INSTEON devices, hot is referred to as line.

While hot is technically only dangerous if you also touch either Neutral or Ground, you are always closer to ground potential than you are to any other electrical potential so Hot will always be dangerous.

Load

Load is the Hot conductor after it has gone through a switch—in other words, load is disconnected when a switch is open (in the "off" position), and connected to hot when a switch is closed (in the "on" position).

Traditional switches are wired only to hot and load, and for this reason there are no neutral wires run to switchboxes in many homes built prior to 1980. In anticipation of smarthome systems such as INSTEON and to standardize the wiring of switch-legs, the National Electrical Ccode changed in the early 1980s to require that neutrals be run to switchboxes.

Neutral or Common

Neutral, often referred to as Common, is the center voltage between the two legs of 220VAC. As such, when connected to either leg it creates a circuit at half voltage, 110VAC. All typical outlets in a home are connected to one of the two 110VAC Hot leads and to neutral.

Neutral is connected to earth ground at the main point of entry electrical panel. This prevents electrical problems in neighboring homes from having any significant impact in your home, ensures that supply power hasn't strayed too far from your house's earth ground to be safe, and ensures that any transient supply voltage is shunted to ground before it enters your home.

While neutral is intended to have 0 volts of potential, this is never actually the case in practice because it forms part of the circuit of every device in the house, and every device draws differing amounts of power. INSTEON devices draw a small amount of operating power from neutral and hot (about 6w) to power their internal circuitry and LEDs.

> Always treat neutral as if it were hot, because you don't know how much electrical potential there is between it and you.

In junction boxes for switches, neutrals are usually unused and wired together into a large bundle with a wire nut. Occasionally you'll see two bundles of neutrals with a wire connecting them because there were too many neutrals for a single wirenut to bind. By code, all unused neutrals in the home must be wired together.

In an outlet junction box, neutrals are wired to the outlets along with hot and ground.

Ground

All electrical power flows to the Earth—it is the zero-voltage reference for all wired electrical circuits. Ground wires create a path for errant power to flow to earth without damaging equipment or shocking humans. The difference between a ground wire and a neutral wire is that ground wires are never intended to carry electrical current as a matter of course and are instead a "safety valve" in the event of a short circuit.

All metal piping systems in the home are connected to earth electrical ground at the MPOE panel, including copper water pipes, gas pipes, and HVAC ducts. This ensures that no unsafe voltage potential can build up and that they shunt any electrical wire that touches them to ground.

In outlets, ground is wired to the third pin of a standard electrical plug. In switchboxes, ground is typically wired to the groundnut on the switch, to the junction box if it is metal, or left free if the junction box is plastic and the switch does not have a groundnut.

It should always be safe to touch a ground wire by definition. If you detect significant (>5v) voltage on a ground wire compared to a known ground such as a water pipe, something is wrong and you should contact a qualified electrician to troubleshoot it.

Circuit wiring

Outlets and lighting are typically wired on separate circuits. While this is not required by code, it is good practice because a device that trips a circuit breaker from over-use is almost always plugged into an outlet, and you don't want to loose lighting when that happens. But there are occasions when it makes sense to put light fixtures and outlets on the same circuit—this is especially common when an outlet is provided at counter-height in the same junction box as a switch.

Most lighting circuits are 15-amp circuits run with 14-gauge wire. Outlets are either 15-amp run with 14-guage wire or 20-amp circuits run with 12-gauge wire, depending on their expected load. Kitchens, bathrooms, and garages are typical places where a 20-amp circuit might be used to power high-draw loads such as microwave ovens, curling irons, and power tools.

In commercial buildings, 15-amp circuits are limited to 8 outlets or fixtures per circuit, and 20-amp circuits are limited to 10. There are no limits for residential wiring according to the NEC, but the commercial limitations are generally adhered to as good practice.

220VAC outlets are typically run on 30 amp breakers using 10-gauge wiring, or may be run on 50 amp breakers using 8-guage wiring for especially heavy loads such as large electrical stoves. Only one outlet can be wired to a 220VAC breaker by code.

Outlets and fixtures on the same circuit are wired in parallel—hot and neutral pass by the load (rather than through it) on their way to the next load so that the circuit is not interrupted or affected by the other loads on the circuit (other than to increase the amount of power drawn overall).

Circuits running to bathrooms must be protected with a Ground Fault Interrupter (GFI), which is an outlet with a fast-blow circuit breaker built into it that can disconnect a circuit faster than the circuit breaker at the panel. This prevents shorts caused by water from electrocuting people who may be wet which makes them better conductors of electricity.

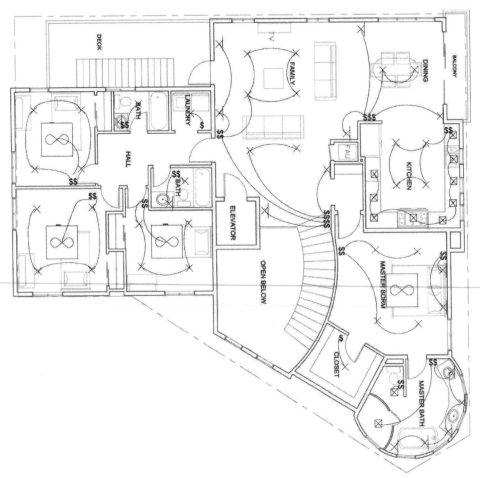

Figure 2.2: Circuit wiring on a blueprint

Switch Wiring

Light fixtures are always wired to switches. Outlets may be, but usually aren't unless the home does not have enough installed fixtures and lamps are necessary.

Switches can be wired two different ways: with the circuit going from the switch to the fixture (referred to as switch-fixture wiring), or from the fixture to the switch (referred to as fixture-switch wiring).

Fixture-Switch

When power is at the fixture, the circuit is brought to the fixture or outlet, and a traveler cable is wired to the switch. The purpose of the traveler wire is to take the hot conductor to the switch and bring it back as the load wire.

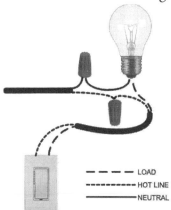

Figure 2.3: Fixture-Switch Wiring

At the fixture, hot is connected to the hot lead of the traveler (and not connected to the fixture), and the fixture's hot is connected to the load wire of the traveler. Hot and load are connected to the switch, so when the switch is closed the circuit is completed and the fixture comes on. Neutral is brought to the switch junction box either as a third conductor or more typically in another cable, and simply capped off (or connected to other neutrals) with a wire nut because it is unused in traditional switch wiring.

Switch-Fixture

When power is at the switch, the circuit is brought to the switch junction box. Neutral is wired through to the cable going to the fixture, and hot is wired to the switch. Load leaves the switch with the cable going to the fixture. At the fixture, neutral and load are wired to the device. This method has the advantage of not requiring an additional cable run to the junction box and in bringing neutral to the switch while still allowing less expensive two-conductor romex to travel from the switch to the fixture, but is less flexible to re-wire than running power to the fixture.

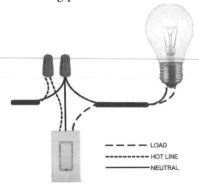

Figure 2.4: Switch-Fixture Wiring

Switch-legs and multi-way switches

Traditional three-way switching, where two wall switches control a single fixture, require special three-way switches in most configurations. The three-way switches are wired to allow power to be routed by either switch, resulting in the typical "switches are the same, light is off—switches are different, light is on" pattern you are used to if you've lived in a home with three-way switching.

Rewiring multi-way switches for INSTEON is an intermediate level skill. Detailed instructions are provided in chapter 6, but you should expect that you might need to call an electrician to get it worked out correctly if you don't have much experience with electrical home wiring.

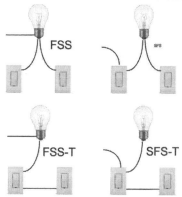

Figure 2.5: Different three-way switch configurations

If you are building a home new construction, tell the electricians not to wire switch-legs or travelers for three-way switches. Be prepared for skepticism, however—I did this, and despite my insistence I still wound up with three three-way switches in my house because my electricians just didn't believe that I knew what I was talking about and "I'd regret it" if I didn't wire three-way circuits. Fortunately they wired them all as Switch-fixture-switch with a traveler, which makes the last traveler easy to simply wire out. I was able to place INSTEON switches in the junction boxes with no loads (the load wire is capped off with a wirenut) to control the devices in exactly the same way.

4-way switches add yet another magnitude of complexity. Suffice it to say that it's not really feasible to wire more than 4-way switching using traditional switches and wiring, which is one of the primary reasons that distributed switching like INSTEON was developed.

Wiring in older homes

Older homes can have substantial electrical wiring differences from the modern wiring described in this chapter.

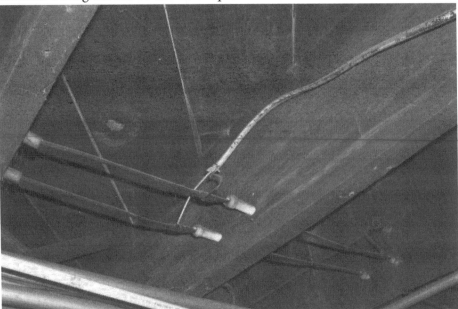

Figure 2.6: Knob & Tube wiring

Knob & Tube wiring: 1880s through 1920s

The oldest homes may have "knob & tube" wiring where separate cloth covered conductors are strung freely through the attic through circular insulators—they might even have bare conductors exposed.

Most rubber cable sheaths developed prior to 1950 will be rotten and brittle today, and unsafe to modify. If you have a home of this age, you should strongly consider upgrading the electrical wiring for your own safety.

> Knob & Tube wiring universally lacks correct grounding.

Although INSTEON will actually operate correctly on home wiring of this age, it may be difficult to install INSTEON devices without damaging your wiring and causing safety issues. Consider using INSTEON plug-in devices and controllers rather than installed devices in homes of this age. In addition to the issues you'll have with knob & tube wiring, you will also have the issues associated with two-conductor wiring described in the next section.

Consider using plug-in controllers such as the ControlLinc or RemoteLinc and plug in responders such as the LampLinc and ApplianceLinc in homes with Knob & Tube wiring. If you also integrate X10 screw-in light-bulb switches for fixtures, you can effectively create a smarthome without touching your electrical wiring.

Two Conductor wiring: 1930s through 1970s

In nearly all homes built prior to the 1980s only two conductors were run to outlets: Hot and Neutral. These homes have outlets with only two vertical slots in the outlet plugs—they lack the third ground hole.

These homes also may lack neutrals run to switches if they are wired "fixture-switch." These switches typically will have only hot and load run to them. Neutral wires stop at the light fixture, and a "traveler"—a two-conductor wire from the fixture to the switchbox—is sent to the switch. One wire of the traveler is connected to hot at the fixture, and the other wire is connected to the load light. At the switchbox, closing the switch connects hot to load, completing the circuit. You can recognize this type of circuit by the single two-conductor cable coming into the junction box with both conductors connected to the switch, and no other wires.

If you're lucky, you may have "switch-fixture" wiring in most switches, which will provide all the wires you need—neutral and hot coming into the switchbox and line and load going to the fixture. If two wires are wired together in the switch junction box, they should be neutrals.

If you have three wires in the box but they are all wired to the switch, you're probably looking at a three-way switch.

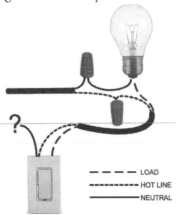

Figure 2.7: 2-wire switch wiring

The problem with two-conductor wiring in switches is that neutrals are not available at the switchbox to power INSTEON devices.

You can still use INSTEON devices in two-conductor homes. Chapter 6 describes how to deal with two conductor switches in simple and effective ways.

Summary

INSTEON devices are easy to install and use—any do-it-yourselfer will be able to install a complete INSTEON system without professional help. Electrical safety is an important concern however—always observe proper safety precautions such as shutting off circuit breakers when working on electrical wiring. If you are unfamiliar with electrical home wiring, have an electrical contractor assist you with your first installations or perform the installation for you.

INSTEON runs over the vast majority of existing home wiring with no modifications. You may require specific INSTEON devices for your particular home wiring needs, but these devices are available. There are a few cases where you may have to perform some additional wiring inside junction boxes and light fixtures in order to get INSTEON devices working correctly, but these cases are easily resolved.

Chapter 3
Understanding INSTEON

If you've read Chapter 1, you know what INSTEON can do. But how does it do it? This chapter covers everything an end-user and installer of INSTEON devices needs to understand about INSTEON in order to design, install, configure, and use INSTEON technology.

> This chapter covers basic INSTEON technology, INSTEON's place amongst competitors in the market, and the basic types of INSTEON devices. If you are already familiar with INSTEON technology, you may want to skip to the next chapter.

INSTEON is: "A distributed control network protocol that operates over powerlines and Radio frequency to create a dual-mesh of peer controls and switches that all repeat signals multiple times for greater reliability. The protocol implements two-way acknowledgement features to ensure that control signals reach their intended destination or the user is warned that they did not." That's easy to write, but what does it all mean? The meaning of that definition is the subject of this chapter.

TERMINOLOGY: CONTROL TECHNOLOGIES

Cross-Link—mutual links that make it possible for multiple devices to control and respond to one another in unison.

Dimmer—An electronic component that can lower the delivered power from maximum to open (off). Electronic dimmers do this by rapidly switching the circuit on and off. The light will "average" the power, and dim as the ratio of "on-time" to "off-time" diminishes. Dimmers are made from solid-state devices called triacs.

Group—A set of INSTEON links that list the responders of a particular INSTEON device's button (or other control group).

ISM—(Industrial, Scientific, and Medical) Reserved radio frequency bands that do not require a license for transmission, which opens them up for unlimited use in short range data networking.

Link—An entry in an INSTEON device's memory that contains the addresses of other devices that it will send control and status messages to.

Microcontroller—a CPU with its own memory and input/output devices onboard—an entire special purpose computer on a single chip.

Network—A group of interconnected devices that can communicate directly with one another by name or address.

Packet—a computer message. Rather than communicating entire volumes of data at once, data is chopped into small packets and individually addressed to the intended recipient. Packet networks allow multiple interleaved conversations to occur simultaneously over a single medium.

Relay—An electronically controlled switch that can connect or interrupt one circuit based on the condition of another circuit. The relay can be a traditional electromechanical relay of the type used in automotive blinkers or a solid-state silicon controlled relay (SCR).

Repeater—A device that listens for signals and then repeats them in a subsequent time frame.

Scene—A concept of control used in home automation controllers that is equivalent to the same group programmed into multiple controllers.

How INSTEON Works

INSTEON technology is designed to avoid the complexity pitfalls that other control networks face:

- Rather than arbitrating access to the network with a complex collision-avoidance protocol in order to prevent devices from talking over one another, INSTEON uses simultaneous transmission to boost signal strength.
- Rather than creating complex routing protocols to determine how signals should be forwarded, all INSTEON devices forward all signals.
- Rather than requiring complex enrollment or individual device address programming, INSTEON devices are assigned a unique address at the factory and need only to be linked in order to begin functioning.

Because INSTEON technology is comparatively simple, all devices can contain the same control circuitry and act as peers. INSTEON devices require no role configuration, enrollment into the system, or definition of masters and slaves.

The next few sections detail exactly what happens from "switch pressed" to "lights on" on an INSTEON network to explain in some depth what is actually happening.

Sending INSTEON commands

All INSTEON devices contain a microcontroller (a complete "computer on a chip") that controls the operation of the device. This controller sends signals over the powerline through a network interface, which is an electronic circuit that connects them to the powerline or radio frequency network. The network interface handles sending packets of information to other microcontrollers on the network.

The process for sending an INSTEON command is simple:

1. The controller sends a broadcast message to all INSTEON devices with its address, group (button) number, and the requested command (On, off, dim, brighten, etc.)

2. All devices on the network examine their link table for an entry from the controller and group. If found, the device will immediately perform the command

3. The controller next sends a peer-to-peer message to each group member individually with the same command request. This guarantees that any device that missed the group broadcast will come on.

4. Each device responds with an acknowledgement. If the controller does not receive an acknowledgement, it will repeat step 3 up to five times.

The following paragraphs describe the process in more detail.

When you press the switch paddle on an INSTEON SwitchLinc, the Microcontroller sends a signal containing its own address and the switch state that the user requested—usually either on, off, dim, or brighten. The message also indicates which button (also called a "group" in Insteon terminology because the button controls a group of responders) on the switch was pressed, so that the various buttons on a multi-button keypad can have different functions.

All INSTEON devices in your home will receive this signal. They each look up the address of the sending device in their table of links, and if they find a match for that device and group (button number), they will perform the requested control command. This way, all the lights in a group can come up instantly and simultaneously.

The original device will then go through its table of links and send an individual ON message to each device linked to that button. This retry ensures that each light comes on. The individual lights all acknowledge this "cleanup" message, which is how the originator knows that every light did indeed come on.

If the original device fails to receive an acknowledgement when it sends the individual command, it will retry up to five times, and then flash a light to indicate that a message was not received.

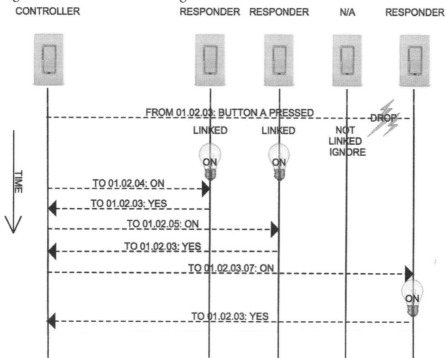

Figure 3.1: Sending an INSTEON control message

The purpose for sending the group broadcast first, rather than simply sending an individual command to each light in the group in order, is due to the low speed at which INSTEON commands travel over the wire. If the controller communicated with each device in order before they came on, a noticeable delay would occur and the lights would come up in order. By sending a group code first, all the lights have the ability to come on immediately and simultaneously, and then any problems that occurred can be cleaned up after the fact. Since problems are rare, this methodology optimizes the responsiveness of the system to human users, but still allows for certainty that lights will come on even when messages are missed.

All devices are repeaters

In addition to listening for control messages, every device that hears the broadcast decreases the hop count number and then retransmits the message simultaneously with all the other devices that heard the message.

Messages would repeat forever if there were no mechanism to have them automatically expire. For that reason, INSTEON messages contain a hop count; a number that is incremented each time a device forwards it. When a message is received that already has the maximum hop count number, it is no longer forwarded. The hop count limits INSTEON messages to five repetitions.

The simultaneous repeating nature of INSTEON is akin to a cheerleader that starts a cheer, which nearby cheerleaders hear and then repeat to the beat, and then the nearby fans repeat it, and soon the entire stadium is repeating the chant. Although you may not have heard the original cheerleader, if you're in the stadium you'll definitely hear the cheer by the end—even if some people are out of sync, saying other things, or fail to repeat the cheer.

The cheering works because it's synchronized to the beat of the cheer itself. The ultimate strength drowns out noise, other signals, and even INSTEON devices that may be slightly out of sync. INSTEON signals are synchronized to the 60Hz power phase, which guarantees that all signals will be repeated in lock step.

INSTEON does not have to develop routing paths to particular devices or keep track of which device to transmit messages to in order to reach some ultimate recipient—All devices simply repeat everything, so all messages eventually get through to their intended recipient.

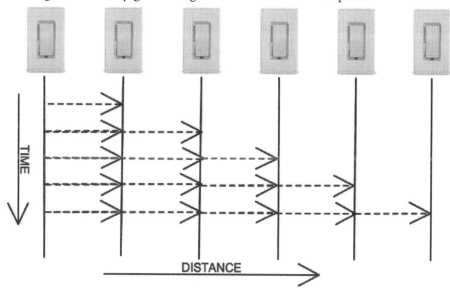

Figure 3.2: Automatic Message Repetition

INSTEON creates a dual-mesh network

INSTEON defines two different media over which its signals can be sent: Wirelessly via radio frequency, and over home electrical powerlines. Because signals are repeated over both types of networks each time they're sent, problems that may occur on one network can be routed around with signals sent over the other. This is why INSTEON Access points are used to bridge the two powerline phases in the home.

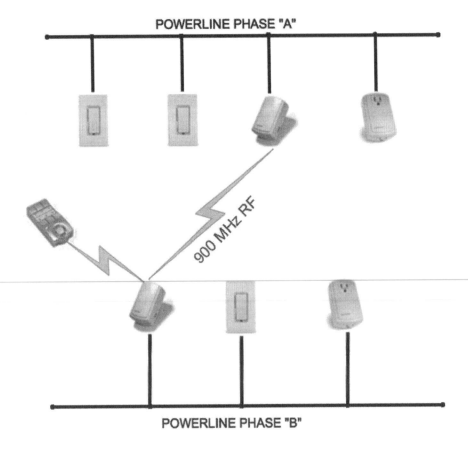

Figure 3.3: A Dual Mesh Network

A mesh network is a network wherein most or all of the devices can participate in forwarding messages, either by routing through a specific predetermined path (as in the case of competing home control wireless technologies Zigbee and Z-Wave) or by repeat broadcasting until all devices have received the signal (as is the case with INSTEON).

Because both RF and powerline INSTEON devices (except battery powered devices) repeat every message they hear, the odds of a message reaching its receiver are dramatically increased: Even though the receiver may not be able to communicate directly with the transmitter, the devices between the two will relay the message between them until the message is received, or a maximum of five relays (or hops) has occurred. This happens automatically across both types of networks.

> If you have a home with older, unreliable electrical wiring, simply add additional INSTEON Access point to improve INSTEON message propagation. If you live in an environment with considerable RF interference, such as near an airport or military base, use a hardwired phase bridge instead. The dual-mesh nature of INSTEON makes it easy to solve problems that bedevil other protocols.

Response

When an INSTEON signal hears a message, in compares the source address to its list of controllers. If they match, then this responder has been previously linked to the sending controller and should listen to the message. The responder interprets the control message and performs the function indicated by the control message—it switches on or off, or to the indicated dim level.

Acknowledgement

The responder waits for the message to stop being transmitted and then transmits an "acknowledgement" which indicates the state that the device changed to. This response is repeated in the same manner as a transmission. If the original sender does not receive a response, it may be programmed to try again or to inform the user that the message was not received—or more likely it will do both in order.

Linking

INSTEON includes special commands for linking. When you press the set button on an INSTEON device, the following actions occur:

1. The first device sends a "set button pressed" message to all INSTEON devices. This informs all INSTEON devices on the network that the sender is looking for group members, or INSTEON devices to add to a particular button's link table. This first device then listens for the "set button pressed" message from other devices.

2. Subsequent devices send a "set button pressed" message to all INSTEON devices. Because the first device is listening for links, it records the addresses of these devices in its link table.

3. The first device then sends a "join group" message to each device that it recorded a link from. Because these devices are now in "set" mode, they record the link from the first device in their link tables. This creates a standard controller-responder link.

4. Subsequent devices then send an acknowledgement to the first device to indicate that they joined the group.

To create a cross-link, the linking process is repeated with the devices reversed.

The linking process creates a web of control between numerous controllers and numerous responders. Most INSTEON devices contain both a controller and a responder, so they can be linked in a number of different ways: As a controller, as a responder, or both as a controller and a responder to another INSTEON device. When both devices are configured as controllers and responders of one another, they are cross-linked, and they will track their load's status across devices and turn on in concert with one another.

Links are stored in the memory of every INSTEON device—not just in a central computer or controller. Since each controller has its own link database, it can send and receive signals without assistance from a PC or home automation controller. This makes INSTEON very reliable because there is no central point of failure.

The complete set of links between INSTEON controllers and responders creates the environment in your home—the multi-way switching, the lighting paths, the scenes, the security triggers, and the environmental controls. The total set of links in all devices is what you create when you configure or program your INSTEON network.

Creating Links using a PC

Creating links can be performed manually on any device, or it can be controlled with a central PC. In practice, you'll manually create links in small installations or when a new inspiration strikes. When performing larger installations or programming sophisticated controllers such as a KeypadLinc, you'll probably want to use a central PC. However, once your programming is complete on the PC, the web of links is downloaded into the INSTEON devices so that the PC is no longer necessary.

Direct Device Control

Computers and home automation controllers can simply directly address devices to control their state without creating links in the devices. This makes it easy for programmers to maintain the state of links in the computer, and make complex decisions about which devices to control and how to control them. However, it also makes the entire system depend on the computer.

> SmartLabs HouseLinc software correctly synchronizes links into INSTEON devices and should be used for large scale programming of INSTEON devices if your home automation controller cannot program INSTEON devices with reconfigured links.

Home automation controllers can also act as technology bridges to connect INSTEON to the data network portion of a smarthome system. This enables control of INSTEON devices to be controlled remotely over the Internet, and to work with your home theater and other systems.

Compatibility

INSTEON message passing also includes provisions for the passing of group messages and for X10 backward compatibility. All INSTEON devices can understand and generate X10 signals if programmed to do so; however, they do not repeat X10 signals and will not make an X10 installation more reliable other than by replacing most X10 devices with INSTEON devices. X10 compatibility makes it easy to begin adding INSTEON devices to your X10 network and smoothly transition one device at a time to a more reliable INSTEON based system.

Basic Types of INSTEON Devices

All INSTEON devices fall into the following categories of devices, based on how they operate. Some are pure controllers and some are pure responders, but most are both controllers and responders.

> Chapter 10 covers the INSTEON devices available at
> the time of this writing in detail.

Phase Couplers

Phase coupling is required in INSTEON installations to allow signals to travel between the two phase-legs in a typical home. Hardwired phase bridges don't have any other functionality, so they are something you'll install and forget—but they are necessary.

If you are building or doing any electrical remodeling, you should strongly consider installing a hard-wired phase coupler. They're the least expensive and most reliable way to couple the phases. Or consider installing a 220VAC plug-in phase coupler on one of your 220V appliance outlets. They are easier to install, but 220VAC outlets are often not easy to get to without moving an appliance.

If a hard-wired phase coupler is not appropriate for your installation, you can use two INSTEON Access Points as RF phase couplers. Access Points also receive signals from RF remotes. You may find reference to SignaLinc RF wireless phase-bridges. They were the original type, but have been replaced by INSTEON Access Points.

Switches

INSTEON switches (called SwitchLincs) replace your existing light switches and locally control the load of the switch they replaced. When you link two SwitchLincs together, they operate in tandem—both loads are controlled by the switch you reprogrammed. You can establish reciprocal links so that both switches control both loads (which you would do in a multi-way switching scenario) or you can leave them so that one switch controls others but is not controlled by them (as you may do in a path lighting scenario).

You can retrofit an existing home for path lighting, multi-way switching, and scene lighting using nothing but SwitchLincs and a phase coupler.

Keypads

INSTEON supports a wide array of keypad controllers, from six and eight button single-gang keypads to in-wall touch screens to tabletop controllers, you can use keypad controllers to put considerable capability at your fingertips. You'll use keypads primarily for multi-way switching, path, and scene lighting.

Remote Controls

Remotes are battery powered handheld controllers, and may be either RF or Infrared (IR). They always have a bridge connected to the INSTEON powerline network to receive the signals and either repeat them onto the powerline or convert them into INSTEON signals, depending upon the technology in use.

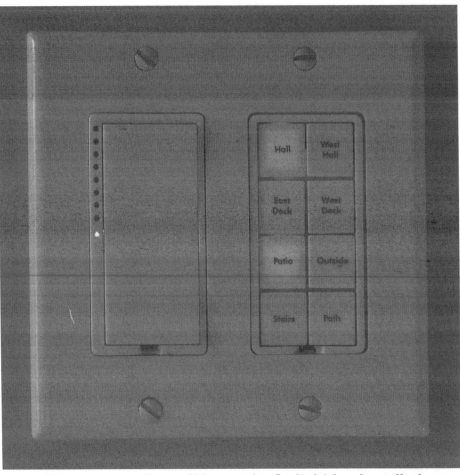

Figure 3.4: A KeypadLinc and a SwitchLinc installed

Technology Bridges

Various INSTEON bridges exist to connect the Powerline network to non-INSTEON controllers such as Infrared remote controls, the Internet, alarm panels, and wireless sensor systems. For example, INSTEON Access Points are a powerline to RF bridge, IRLinc is an infrared to INSTEON bridge, and SmartLinc is an Internet to INSTEON bridge.

Powerline Modems and Powerline Controllers

Powerline Modems and Controllers are bridges that adapt INSTEON signals to common computer interfaces such as RS-232 serial and USB. PLMs and PLCs are the basis of nearly all other technology bridges because they give developers an easy way to interface to INSTEON using existing protocols and tools. PLCs are PLMs with additional memory and the ability to run a small amount of custom program code.

Computers

With the addition of a Powerline Modem (PLM) or Powerline Controller (PLC), any computer can become an INSTEON controller. This enables any level of sophistication in scene management and device control.

Relays

Relays are INSTEON devices that turn power on or off to any type of appliance. Relays can be part of an INSTEON switch, can sit between the device and the outlet, can replace the outlet, or can be wired in line with the controlled appliance depending on the particular need. Some INSTEON devices are referred to as "ON/OFF" devices—this term is synonymous with Relay.

Timers

Timers are relays that include a timing circuit to turn them off after a specific period of time, which may be indicated by preprogramming, by tapping the switch a number of times, or by pressing a key that indicates how long the device should remain on. Timers are used in rooms that are not normally occupied to ensure that lights don't remain on indefinitely.

Dimmers

Dimmers are a special case of relay that can provide a percentage of power to incandescent lights instead of being limited to on/off operation. They should not be used with inductive loads such as fans or other magnetic loads, or fluorescent lighting. These loads can be damaged by dimmers and will cause premature failure of the dimmer itself.

I/O Controllers

I/O Controllers are a type of technology bridge designed to detect inputs from relay-type sensors that cause a short when they are sensing, or to drive low-voltage loads such as sprinkler valves or bells. I/O Controllers connect INSTEON to a wide variety of devices.

Sensors

Sensors detect a state in the environment and send a control signal based on the state or change of state. Motion sensors are a common type of sensor. Many non-INSTEON sensors can be bridged to an INSTEON network through an I/O controller, but a few sensors are directly available as INSTEON devices.

Comparing INSTEON

A useful way to learn about a system is to compare it to other similar systems. The remainder of this chapter compares INSTEON to the various other home automation technologies that are available as of this writing.

> If you've already decided to use INSTEON technology and aren't interested in its history or place amongst competitors, you can skip the remainder of this chapter.

Types of Home Control systems

There are two basic types of home control systems:
- Central lighting systems
- Distributed control systems

Central lighting systems bring all the lighting wiring to a central point in the home and use a large array of load switching panels to control everything using a single computer. They are somewhat similar to alarm panels in their functional design except that they include electronics to handle much larger switched voltages than an alarm panel has to deal with.

Distributed control systems work with traditionally wired homes and operate by replacing traditional light switches with microcontrollers that operate on a network that either runs over the electrical wiring or is wireless using radio frequency in the ISM bands.

All types of lighting control systems have advantages and drawbacks.

Central Control Systems

Central control systems centralize all the power switching in large panels in a single location in the home. Every light—not just every lighting circuit—has it's own home run to these switching panels. Every switch in the house also has its own home-run low-voltage cable running to the lighting system control units.

The central panels are then programmed to match a specific switch button input to a particular set of lights (a path or scene) that should be turned on or dimmed.

Central lighting systems are considered in the industry to be "premium" lighting solutions: While expensive, they provide perfect control, reliable switching with no technology related trade-offs (other than that they only control lighting), and high reliability.

However, central lighting systems require that the entire home be specially wired—both in the fact that every light must be wired to the control panel, and the fact that switches must be wired using specialty wiring. For this reason, central lighting switches cannot be retrofit into existing homes without a complete electrical replacement as part of a remodel.

There are also problems with controlling lamps and other free standing appliances—outlets are generally not wired to the central lighting system because there's no way to tell what will be plugged into them, so freestanding lamps aren't part of the home control system. You can't easily change a load type from a light to a ceiling fan or fluorescent light unless the load is exactly the same as the system was built to handle in that particular location. Putting an inductive load on a dimmed circuit for example can damage the load and the control panel. This problem keeps centralized lighting systems focuses exclusively on lighting and not able to incorporate other elements of home control.

Because the central control panels are expensive, the wiring is specialized and increases costs, and the installers require special skill. For these reasons, centralized lighting systems are simply not an option for most people. That's why their market has been strictly limited to new luxury homes. The various vendors have been forced to price their products for that specific market, thus preventing much penetration into the typical home market.

Distributed Control Systems

Distributed control systems do not centralize the power switching. Rather, they work the way traditionally wired systems work, but they automate the function of the switch.

Fault tolerance starts with de-centralization. Distributed systems such as the Internet are far better able to tolerate the loss of a few components than centralized systems like the obsolete mainframe computers of old. In the same way, a decentralized control system can better tolerate the loss of a component than a centralized system.

The major distributed control systems developed for home use are:
- X-10
- UPB (Universal Powerline Bus)
- Z-Wave
- Zigbee
- INSTEON

These technologies will all be discussed and compared in the following section. They all share a number of common features:
- Signal distribution by powerline, wireless in the ISM bands, or both
- A system of controllers, responders, and repeaters to transmit, receive, and strengthen signals
- A very similar set of available devices.

They are differentiated primarily by cost and reliability.

TERMINOLOGY: DISTRIBUTED CONTROL SYSTEMS

Responder—performs load control. Responders listen for commands, and switch the load based on the received command. The switches are either relays, dimmers or specialized I/O devices.

Controller—sends commands to the responder. Most protocols support combined controller/responders that locally control a particular load and also transmit commands to other responders.

Bridge—passes commands from wireless devices to wired devices, or converts commands from one type of control system to another (for example, to a security system). Bridges may simply resend received data on another type of network, for example from radio to powerline, or they may receive a signal on one network or protocol, match that command in a conversion table, and resend the converted command on another network or protocol.

Interface—adapts the protocol to general-purpose computers so that the automation system can be controlled by computer software. These automation controllers adapt the protocol to some computer interface, such as serial, USB, or Ethernet, and provide a way for software programs to directly control the home automation system.

X-10

The first home automation system developed was X-10, which was developed in 1975 by Pico Electronics. X-10 transmits communication signals over the power lines, so it requires no special wiring. X-10 is now an open industry standard. It remains the least expensive and most popular home automation system, and dozens of manufacturers make thousands of different X-10 compatible devices.

> INSTEON devices are backward compatible with X-10 devices and can control and be controlled by them because INSTEON devices "speak" X-10 protocol in addition to INSTEON protocol. X-10 devices cannot receive INSTEON messages however.

X-10 systems consist of controllers and responders. A controller sends commands, and a responder or device module responds to commands. Examples of device modules include plug-in on/off appliance controllers, screw-in lamp dimmers, and I/O controllers.

X-10 communications exploits the fact that household electrical wiring is relatively quiet during the moment when the AC signal transitions across the zero voltage boundaries 60 times per second. In that instant, an X-10 device can transmit one "bit," or binary digit, of information. The information that X-10 sends is usually an address of the device being controlled, and a command.

An X-10 packet consists of a 4-bit house code, a 4-bit unit code, and a 4-bit command code. This provides 256 uniquely addressable devices (4-bits of house code + 4-bits of unit code=8-bits, $2^8=256$). The commands are typically On, Off, and dim level, although the command can be anything that the receiving device can interpret. A controller can transmit multiple unit codes before sending a command, and this will cause all the receivers to react to the command instantly.

House codes are important because the high-frequency carrier signal used by X-10 can pass through power pole transformers, making X-10 codes appear on the electrical wiring of nearby homes, which could cause unintentional interference with a neighbor's X-10 devices. A better solution is to use inductive filters at the main point of entry to attenuate X-10 signals as they pass in and out of the house. These are known as powerline filters, and they are a common component of professional X-10 installations.

Other than neighbors, there's nothing to prevent one from using multiple house codes in a single home—however, you cannot send a single command to units in more than one house code, so house codes effectively equal groups in X-10.

X-10 repeats each command twice to improve reliability and improve immunity to noise. However, there is no acknowledgement from the receiver that a command has been acted upon.

X-10 also implements a radio frequency protocol that operates at 310MHz in the U.S. and 433MHz in Europe. An X-10 receiver bridges received signals onto the powerline system.

> HomeLink garage door controllers, built into most luxury cars, can learn and transmit RF X-10 signals. You can integrate this functionality into your INSTEON network using an EZX-10RF bridge.

Problems with X-10

X-10 originally had a number of problems related to signal propagation through house lines, such as signals not transiting across the two power phases, signal propagation between separate homes, and transient line noise caused by inductive loads such as transformers and motors. These problems would cause the installation of some installations to be so unreliable as to be useless.

These problems have largely been solved by the introduction of phase couplers, noise filters, and signal repeaters, but significant problems remain.

X-10 controllers will transmit on the line even when another command is being transmitted—the two commands then become garbled. Because it takes quite a bit of time (more than half a second) to transmit a single X-10 command, the likelihood that two people will initiate a command at the same is actually quite high. Worse, an X-10 command that starts after another controller has transmitted an address but before the command starts can actually override the command with the command of the second device and cause the wrong operation to occur.

X-10 responders do not acknowledge to the controller that the command has been received and acted upon, so the user will only know if the command has been completed if what they wanted to have happen actually occurred. Often times this is not obvious.

X-10 can support only 256 devices, which is an easy number to reach in a completely automated home. Because devices are individually addressed, large scenes are slow to deploy causing a very noticeable delay in lighting. Support for arbitrary dimming is primitive compared to more modern protocols.

These problems combine to create more than a 1% failure case for X-10 devices in a system that works well, and about 25% in bad cases. Lights that don't switch on and Garage doors that open randomly create a strong sense of unreliability in the minds of users and have severely limited the adoption of X-10 amongst non-technical users.

Universal Powerline Bus

Universal Powerline Bus was the first major competitor to X-10 to achieve any real market success. It has been on the market about five years longer than INSTEON and Z-Wave.

UPB operates in a manner similar to X-10, but using a fundamentally different method of creating signals on the powerline. It is more reliable than X-10 and twice as fast.

UPB isn't nearly as fast or reliable as INSTEON, however, and it lacks the range of device support that INSTEON has. Furthermore, UPB is not considered to be "user-installable" by its own industry because it requires special tools and software to configure the UPB devices. The manufacturer recommends certified installers and there is very little support for purchasing UPB devices directly without purchasing them through an installer who will mark them up.

UPB has serious problems with dimmers because dimmers work by "chopping" the AC powerline signal—and these "chops" look a lot like UPB messages. UPB dimmers avoid the problem by not getting too dim, but a traditional dimmer anywhere in the house can jam the entire UPB system if it's on a dim setting.

UPB devices cost about twice as much as equivalent INSTEON devices.

> INSTEON and UPB do not interfere with one another—you can successfully use both over the same powerlines, although they cannot control one another directly. UPB will have problems with INSTEON dimmers however.

Z-Wave

Z-Wave is a distributed control system very similar to INSTEON in terms of the available devices and capabilities of the system, but which transmits its control signals over wireless in the 900MHz ISM band (similar to the INSTEON-RF protocol) rather than over electrical home wiring. Z-Wave and INSTEON-RF transmit on different "channels" in the 900MHz ISM band and do not interfere with one another.

Z-Wave devices automatically create an RF-mesh network amongst themselves, and every powerline device (some are battery operated) acts as a repeater of Z-Wave signals in exactly the same way that INSTEON repeats powerline signals. Signal repetition solves the problems of distant devices for Z-Wave for the same reason. Each Z-Wave device has a nominal transmission distance of between 20' in constricted areas to 100' in free space areas, with the vendor recommending that devices be placed every 30' at maximum to ensure good coverage.

Z-Wave requires a central controller, usually in the form of a remote control, to manage the routing of Z-Wave signals. The controller is also used to enroll and link devices into the network. Z-Wave routing is determined by the master controller but is self-healing, with devices able to find paths around damaged devices. Z-Wave routing is actually phenomenally complicated, but handled entirely automatically by the devices themselves. The complexity is not apparent to end users, but it does increase the cost of the circuits that perform the work.

There is actually one case where the routing complexity of Z-Wave is apparent to users: When you want to change something. Moving any Z-Wave device requires you to un-enroll it and re-enroll it so that the master controller can determine its new position in the network and create new routing paths.

Un-enrolling can be very problematic: If a Z-Wave device disappears from the network (because it failed, you unplugged it, a circuit-breaker is off, or what have you) the Z-Wave devices attempting to control it will retry for up to seven seconds—often times being completely unresponsive during that period. Furthermore, you have to press a button on a Z-Wave device to un-enroll it from the network. If the device failed or is no longer available to be wired back in, all devices that control it will be subject to this very long pause behavior. The standard solution is to factory reset all controllers and re-enroll all devices—in other words, start over completely. It's a pretty bad failure mode that is caused by the complexity of the network routing protocol used in Z-Wave.

Theoretically, because of the placement criteria and the 4-hop maximum repetition, larger houses (over 5,000 sq.ft.) would be a problem for Z-Wave and would at a minimum require more careful planning. In practice, there are very few houses too large for Z-Wave, although most commercial buildings would be.

The primary competitive problem for Z-Wave is cost. While the Z-Wave consortium has done a good job of making RF devices inexpensive, they still cost nearly twice as much as the comparable INSTEON device. That makes a large installation cost a large amount more than the equivalent INSTEON installation.

As with any RF device, problems of interference, reception, and propagation throughout a home are possible in some installations and difficult to detect without testing. That said, Z-Wave by all accounts is more reliable than X-10 and probably about as reliable as INSTEON. These problems vary widely depending on the size of the home, the distance between devices, the number of devices, and the type of home construction. Older homes with plaster-wire walls and grounded metal back boxes, which are common, can cause serious problems for Z-Wave devices.

Zigbee

Zigbee is an open standard for communication amongst low power control devices. Based loosely on the Bluetooth specification used in cell phone headsets and wireless computer mice (amongst other things) and operating in either the 900MHz or 2.4GHz ISM band, Zigbee devices are lower power, lower battery consumption, and lower range than Z-Wave devices. At the time of this writing, only an insignificant number of Zigbee devices exist and it is not yet possible to predict how well Zigbee will compete against Z-Wave and INSTEON in the market.

Zigbee was originally designed to be a less expensive, lower powered, and more specific version of Bluetooth for applications where the features and expense of Bluetooth weren't necessary but a routing protocol was. Unfortunately, Bluetooth is now mature and inexpensive, and Zigbee still isn't really on the market. Bluetooth doesn't define a routing protocol however, so it cannot act as a home automation control protocol.

Zigbee will have similar problems to Z-Wave based on the fact that it is RF based, requires device enrollment, and uses sophisticated routing protocols and master/slave devices. In fact, because it is a lower-power protocol, it is likely that it will have more problems than Z-Wave in reception reliability.

One big strike against Zigbee is its failure to get out of the gate—its already in it third major revision and no significant market yet exists. The first generation of Zigbee devices isn't even compatible with the second generation because the specification was essentially incomplete. The third generation is backward compatible with the second, however.

Zigbee and INSTEON operate on different channels in the 900MHz ISM band do not interfere with one another.

The History of INSTEON

SmartLabs, a large manufacturer of X-10 devices, developed INSTEON specifically as a follow-on replacement for X-10. X-10 had been a really good idea—many of the things it enabled could not be effectively accomplished using any other technology available at the time. But after thirty years, no technology will continue to compete well without being updated.

X-10 compatibility was considered to be a key feature, both to drive adoption amongst X-10 users and to retain the large market of esoteric X-10 devices that would likely not be available in an INSTEON compatible version until adoption was at least as high as X-10.

Why replace X-10 with something similar? Because INSTEON corrects or largely mitigates all the problems that plagued X-10 without significantly increasing costs.

There was no standard way to couple the powerline phases in X-10—it was an exercise left to the installer, and uninformed users may have never understood that phase coupling was important. INSTEON emphasizes phase coupling and provides retrofit phase couplers as a standard part of all starter packages. Furthermore, the instructions for all INSTEON devices point out the necessity of phase couplers clearly.

INSTEON devices automatically repeat every signal they hear in the next signal window. This means that a signal becomes stronger every time its repeated throughout the house and virtually guarantees that even distant devices will receive the signal correctly.

> As the number of INSTEON devices increases, the reliability of the INSTEON network increases.

INSTEON devices acknowledge the receipt of signals, so if a signal fails to reach its intended responder, the controller can repeat the signal or at least alert the user with a flashing light or other signal to warn them.

INSTEON devices are pre-addressed at the factory with a unique address. Not only is no programming required, address conflicts are not possible.

INSTEON is more than 10 times faster than X-10 in practice, reducing the likelihood of signal collisions and increasing the number of commands (and therefore size of home) that can be effectively controlled.

Finally, INSTEON devices are backward compatible with X-10, and can be configured to control or respond to X-10 signals. X-10 compatibility allows uses to make use of obscure and small-market X-10 devices that may never be manufactured in an INSTEON version, as well as providing a migration path from X-10 to INSTEON without requiring every device to be replaced at once.

Summary

INSTEON is a home automation control protocol that allows a network of peer controllers and responders to communicate over powerline and radio frequency to act in concert as a unified lighting, appliance, and environment control system.

INSTEON devices automatically repeat all messages that they hear simultaneously—creating a "louder" broadcast throughout the home with each retransmission and new device that joins in the "chorus." This virtually guarantees that the responder will hear the controller irrespective of their distance from one another, noise on the line, or other impediments to signaling.

Other competing distributed control network protocols exist, but they are either considerably more expensive or considerably less reliable. INSTEON has a complete range of home automation devices available and works well in homes of any size.

Chapter 4
Starting Out with INSTEON

Firstly, don't worry about designing for INSTEON. Besides the installation of a phase bridge, which can be as simple as plugging in two Access Points, there are no system requirements you need to worry about beyond purchasing the devices to do exactly what you want.

> INSTEON is nearly design-free. You don't have to know or do anything beyond solving your immediate requirements other than to install an inexpensive phase bridge.

Don't expect to come up with every possible use for your system or pre-program it entirely in advance—one of the major features of INSTEON (especially when compared to its competitors) is how easy it is to redefine your uses after the system is installed. Nothing in your INSTEON design need be permanent; don't worry about getting everything right the first time. As you get a feel for your system, you will certainly come up with more uses for it.

If you are building new or performing a complete electrical remodel, you should strongly consider using INSTEON switches for all of your installed lighting. Although INSTEON switches cost more than manual switches, the cost savings you can realize through simpler wiring may offset much of the cost.

TERMINOLOGY: INSTEON LANGUAGE

Accessory buttons—buttons on controllers that do not control the local load. On a 6-button KeypadLinc, the On and Off buttons control the local load, while the A/B/C/D buttons are accessory buttons. On an 8-button KeypadLinc, the A button controls the local load in Toggle Mode and the B/C/D/E/F/G/H buttons are accessory buttons.

Cross-Link—the state of two controller-responders configured so that they have reciprocal links to each other. When a cross-link exists, the devices will correctly maintain on/off and brightness levels matching the controlled load. When cross-links are not configured, LEDs on the controller indicate the status of the last button press and may not match the status of the device.

Link—an entry in an INSTEON controller that defined the address and other parameters of a device that it controls, so that when the controller is activated, it can send a message to the receiver to perform the action it received. INSTEON controllers can be linked to multiple receivers so that a single action controls multiple devices.

Non-Toggle Mode—methods of operation for KeypadLinc accessory buttons that cause the button to always send an ON (or OFF) command. These modes are useful when buttons cannot be cross-linked.

Toggle Mode—a method of operation for KeypadLinc accessory buttons that cause the button to maintain an on/off state (indicated by the LED). When the LED is lit, the button will send an OFF command if pressed, and when unlit it will send an ON command. Toggle Mode is the default mode of operation and should be used when an individual light can be cross-linked to the button.

If you aren't performing a complete rebuild, you'll probably want to start small and grow your system room-by-room. There's no penalty or extra work involved in growing an INSTEON system piece-by-piece. You won't have to start over with your existing programming, call out a service technician, or go through a lengthy device enrollment process when you add a new device to your system. Growing your system device-by-device ensures that you'll spend the bare minimum to get what you want.

Because my home was new construction, I did perform very heavy predictive planning—but I went overboard by purchasing devices beyond the installed switches that we had to have up front. You only need to have wired-in devices in advance. Don't buy advanced items such as Web Controllers and TimerLincs until you've got your initial wired-in devices working and settled.

Over time, I've moved about 30% of my switches in order to swap relays and dimmers, move the location of timers, install KeypadLincs in places where we hadn't predicted we'd need them, and remove them from places where they weren't being used. I wound up deleting the links I setup originally, creating new ones that actually match how we use the system, and ordering new laser-etched buttons for about half of the buttons on our KeypadLincs. I also have plenty of "spare" INSTEON devices that I didn't wind up needing for problems I chose to solve a different way. Save yourself the hassle and money by starting small and growing your system organically as you come up with uses for it.

> I spent about $5000 on INSTEON devices (perhaps $1000 of which I turned out not to really need) for a 6000 sq.ft. home, and saved about $2500 on the electrical contracting and wiring due to simpler requirements.

Getting started

The first thing you need to do to get started with INSTEON is to install a phase bridge. You have four options:

- A pair of INSTEON Access Point plug-in wireless phase bridges. This is the easiest possible solution.
- Two INSTEON Access Points. Easy to install and provides the ability to link to INSTEON wireless devices, but also the most expensive.

- SignaLinc plug-in 220v phase bridge. An easy and highly reliable option.
- SignaLinc hardwired phase-bridge. The most reliable and least expensive, but also the most difficult to install.

A WIRELESS INSTEON System

WHAT YOU NEED

⇒ Two INSTEON Access Points (#2443P).

WHAT TO DO

⇒ Plug one Access Point or SignaLinc into each of the two phases of your home electrical wiring.

AN EASY AND ECONOMICAL INSTEON System

WHAT YOU NEED

⇒ One plug-in phase bridge #4816A2 or #4816B2.

WHAT TO DO

⇒ Install between your electrical dryer and 220VAC outlet.

THE MOST RELIABLE INSTEON System

WHAT YOU NEED

⇒ One hardwired phase bridge #2406H

WHAT TO DO

⇒ Install the phase bridge at your circuit breaker panel

Solving a specific lighting problem

There are a number of specific problems you can solve with INSTEON without replacing every installed switch in your house. INSTEON technology is a great enabler for do-it-yourselfers who want to improve or change the function of electrical switches.

Solving a specific problem with INSTEON is a great way to "get your feet wet" with INSTEON before committing a lot of time and money to purchasing INSTEON devices for your entire home. You'll be able to prove to yourself how well INSTEON works and be certain that it will meet your requirements before you spend a lot of money on it.

The next few sections cover a number of situations where installing just a few INSTEON devices makes sense.

Lamp control

The simplest problem INSTEON will help you solve is automating the control of lamps in your living room. By purchasing an Access Point, a RemoteLinc, and a LampLinc dimmer for each of your lamps you can remotely control each lamp in your living room from wherever you sit, without retrofitting anything in your home or touching your electrical wiring in any way. If you are looking for an easy and convenient way to test INSTEON, this is it.

WIRED LAMP CONTROL

WHAT YOU NEED

⇒ One ControlLinc plug-in Insteon controller (#2430)

⇒ A LampLinc Lamp dimmer for each lamp you wish to control (#2456D3)

WHAT TO DO

⇒ Link each LampLinc Dimmer to the ControlLinc plug-in Insteon controller.

⇒ Link to different buttons to control lamps individually, or link multiple lamps to the same button to control them as a group, creating scenes.

WIRELESS LAMP CONTROL

WHAT YOU NEED

⇒ An INSTEON Access Point (#2443) (Not necessary if you already have Access Points as phase bridges—however, The RemoteLinc does not work with SignaLinc RF phase bridges)

⇒ One RemoteLinc Wireless remote control (#2440)

⇒ A LampLinc Lamp Dimmer for each lamp you wish to control (#2456D3)

⇒ Link the RemoteLinc buttons to each LampLinc.
⇒ Link to different buttons to control lamps individually, or link multiple lamps to the same button to control them as a group, creating scenes.

Creating a virtual multi-way switch

The simplest wired-in INSTEON problem to solve is the multi-way switch. All you need to do is replace the light switch for the light(s) you want to control with an INSTEON SwitchLinc, and replace the light switches that you want to use to control it with SwitchLincs.

If all you want to do is create a virtual three-way switch in a single room, it's likely that all your circuits will be on the same phase and you can get away with not installing a phase bridge. However, if any of the devices doesn't seem to work when you try to link it, you'll need to install a phase bridge to solve the problem. Also be aware that you won't get away with expanding your INSTEON system much beyond one room without installing a phase bridge.

Be aware that installed INSTEON switches always control their local load—the light or appliance that the original switch controlled. For example, let's say you have a long hallway that has only one light switch at one end. But there's a room with a center light fixture at the other end of the hallway, and you would like to use that switch to control the hallway light. If you replace the room light with a SwitchLinc, you can configure that SwitchLinc to control both the room light and the hall light, but you cannot configure it to control the hall light alone.

The correct solution in situation is to use a 6-button KeypadLinc to control the room light fixture. This way, the primary load (the room fixture) can be controlled using the "on/off" buttons, and the hall light can be controlled using one of the A/B/C/D buttons (or two of them if you want to create separate on/off buttons rather than a toggle button).

WHAT YOU NEED

⇒ An INSTEON SwitchLinc (#2476D) to replace the switch for each light you wish to control

⇒ An INSTEON KeypadLinc 6-button Dimmer (#2486DWH6) for each switch location you wish to control the light from.

WHAT TO DO

⇒ Replace the switch that currently controls the light with an INSTEON SwitchLinc dimmer (for incandescent lights) or relay (for florescent lights).

⇒ Replace each switch at locations where you would like to control the light with an INSTEON KeypadLinc 6-button Dimmer. If you want this switch location's local load to also come on, you can use a typical SwitchLinc.

⇒ Program the A, B, C, or D accessory button on each KeypadLinc to control the SwitchLinc attached to the light. Now the KeypadLincs on/off buttons will control their local light, and the accessory button will control the multi-way light.

Moving a switch

A common problem with electrical installations in a home is that switches often wind up where they would be convenient for the original builder rather than where they would be convenient for the user. In my house, we have a light switch below a wall sconce, but the switch is placed next to a door that nobody will ever use because it goes out to a small balcony.

By linking that switch to the main living room recessed lights, we can use that light without having to walk across the living room to it all the time.

Placing a KeypadLinc next to the primary entrance to a room is a great way to control all the room lighting conveniently irrespective of where the wall switches are actually located. You can put lamps and other movable lights on them as well.

LINKING OR MOVING SWITCHES

⇒ Use the procedure above entitled "Multi-Way Switches"

A single path of lights

Path lighting in a home is really useful—but the architecture of many homes create only one or perhaps two paths that would ever need to be controlled as a path. In these cases, you need only replace the switches that control the lights involved to create a single path of lights. You can use a switch at both ends of the path to turn the entire path on or off, or use a KeypadLinc at both ends to create path on/off buttons.

PATH LIGHTING

WHAT YOU NEED

⇒ An INSTEON SwitchLinc (#2476D) to replace the switch for each light you wish to participate in the path.
⇒ Two INSTEON KeypadLinc 6-button Dimmers (#2486DWH6) for the locations at the beginning and end of the path where you will turn on and turn off the path.

WHAT TO DO

⇒ Install the KeypadLincs at both "ends" of the path. For example, if you want to turn the path on when you enter the house, replace the first switch you come to when you enter the house with a KeypadLinc. If the path ends in the master bedroom, place the other KeypadLinc at that location.
⇒ Replace all switches participating in the path with SwitchLincs appropriate for their load type.
⇒ Program a non-toggle mode "Path On" button at the entry way by linking each SwitchLinc to the KeypadLinc. Do the same for a "Path Off" button at the end of the path. Use the instructions that come with the KeypadLinc to perform the conversion to non-toggle mode for the path buttons.

Solving hard-to-reach problems

Pull-chain lights, retrofitted attic vent fans, and plug-in lamps and appliances usually don't come with easy-to-reach wall switches. Often you have to stumble through a dark room to turn the lights on.

INSTEON makes it trivial to use LampLincs, ApplianceLincs, and InLineLinc relays and dimmers to turn any light switch into a control for these kinds of problems. InLineLincs allow you to control fixtures and permanently installed appliances that lack wall switches. LampLincs and ApplianceLincs are plug-in adapters that control power to the appliance or lamp plugged into them.

SWITCH CONTROL FOR A PULL CHAIN LIGHT

WHAT YOU NEED

⇒ An INSTEON InLineLinc Relay installed above the pull-chain light fixture in the ceiling.
⇒ One INSTEON KeypadLinc 6-button Dimmer (#2486DWH6) to replace a light switch at the location where you would like to control the pull-chain lighting fixture.

WHAT TO DO

⇒ Install a KeypadLinc 6-Button Dimmer or On/Off switch near the light.
⇒ Remove the fixture in the ceiling and wire in an INSTEON InLineLinc Relay or Dimmer. Do not complete the installation.
⇒ Link the KeypadLinc to the InLineLinc manually before completing the installation. Alternately, you can record the InLineLinc address and perform the programming using HouseLinc if you have it.
⇒ Complete the installation by placing the InLineLinc relay in the ceiling above the figure, replacing the light fixture, and leaving the light's pull-chain in the on position.

SWITCHED CONTROL FOR A PLUG-IN FAN

WHAT YOU NEED

⇒ One INSTEON KeypadLinc 6-button Dimmer #2486DWH6 to replace a light switch at the location where you would like to control the fan.

⇒ One INSTEON ApplianceLinc #2456S3 installed between the fan and the outlet.

WHAT TO DO

⇒ Install the KeypadLinc at the entry to the room.
⇒ Unplug the fan, plug it into an ApplianceLinc Relay, and plug the ApplianceLinc Relay into the wall.
⇒ Link the ApplianceLinc relay to an accessory button on the KeypadLinc.

Controlling Holiday lighting with INSTEON

The typical way to control holiday lighting is with mechanical plug-in timers. You put one on everything you plug in, and the lights come on and go off at the time specified on their individual timer.

INSTEON gives you a lot more control. Using either a TimerLinc plug-in timer or the Events feature of HouseLinc in combination with an ApplianceLinc or LampLinc plugged in to each of your lighting displays, you can customize the timing of your display to come on at sunset or to fade on and off slowly. You can also easily override your timers from any switch in the house to bring the lights on instantly when guests arrive or turn them all off manually at night.

If you celebrate Christmas, set the Christmas tree lights to come on based on a motion sensor for Christmas morning so the tree lights up when the little ones enter the room. You can set the motion sensor to bring up your bedroom lights as well, so you know when they're up and about.

Whatever you decide to do, the ability to extend lighting control to all of your holiday lighting displays and managing them as a single group will make your life easier and save power.

CONTROL HOLIDAY LIGHTING

WHAT YOU NEED

⇒ TimerLinc
⇒ ApplianceLinc relay for outside lights or lights that don't require dimming

WHAT TO DO

⇒ Setup the TimerLinc to send an ON command at sundown, and an off command at midnight or an appropriate time to turn holiday lights off.

⇒ Connect the first string of lights to the TimerLinc, and each subsequent string of lights to an ApplianceLinc.

⇒ Link each Appliance Link to the TimerLinc by pressing the TimerLinc's set button for three seconds, and then pressing the set button on the ApplianceLinc. All the ApplianceLincs will now come on in unison with the TimerLinc based on its timer programming.

CONTROL CHRISTMAS TREE LIGHTING

WHAT YOU NEED

⇒ LampLinc dimmer for lighting displays you want to fade on or off

⇒ An INSTEON motion sensor

WHAT TO DO

⇒ Plug your Christmas tree lights into a LampLinc and link it to an INSTEON motion sensor.

⇒ Set a custom ramp rate on the LampLinc by dimming the LampLinc (with dimmer corresponding to a slower ramp rate) and then pressing the set button on the LampLinc twice. The return to the motion sensor controller and press its set button for three seconds. Now your tree lights will fade on when someone enters the room.

⇒ Link your bedroom lights to the same INSTEON motion sensor.

Security with INSTEON

INSTEON I/O Controllers and motion detectors or EZSnsRF bridges from SimpleHomeNet are all you need to create a simple security system that can be retrofitted into any home. Using wireless battery operated motion detectors and door closure detectors, the EZSnsRF turns security events into INSTEON commands that you can use to turn on a warning light, buzzer, patio light, or buzzer.

You can use EZIO outputs or an I/OLinc to sound an electric chime, direct a pan-tilt-zoom camera towards detected motion, or trigger the inputs on any traditional alarm panel. EZIO devices can also be wired to a myriad of existing security sensors such as motion sensors, glass breakage detectors, window and door closure sensors, and light detectors. By creating INSTEON events in reaction to these sensors, you can bring up lights or control any aspect of your smarthome.

INSTEON motion sensors send an on command, and then after a delay, an off command. This can be problematic if you are controlling a light that is already on—the signal to turn it on will have no effect, but the signal to shut off will turn the light off, which may tend to annoy anyone using the light. INSTEON motion sensors can be programmed to only send an on command to mitigate this problem.

A SIMPLE HOME SECURITY SYSTEM

WHAT YOU NEED

⇒ Any Insteon controlled lighting, or an I/OLinc Remote Chime Alert kit
⇒ One SimpleHomeNet EZSnsRF Dakota to Insteon Bridge (#31275) or an Access Point
⇒ A Dakota Wireless motion sensor or INSTEON motion sensor for each area you want to monitor (#7315)

WHAT TO DO

⇒ Install the EZSnsRF Dakota to Insteon Bridge on any electrical outlet in your home.
⇒ Link the Dakota Wireless Motion Sensor to the EZSnsRF Dakota bridge using the instructions that come with the EZSnsRF bridge.
⇒ Link the EZSnsRF bridge to the INSTEON lights or the I/OLinc Remote Chime Alert Kit that you would like to be activated when motion is detected.

There are limits to what you can accomplish with this type of simple security system: You can only alert on any single trigger. If you'd like to combine a series of triggers, or negate a trigger based on the value of another trigger (such as a "disarm system" button) you'll need an actual alarm panel or a home automation controller to combine the inputs for you.

The Smart Entertainment Center

INSTEON can't transmit video or audio throughout your home, but it can dim the lights when you start a movie or allow you to control lighting from your universal remote.

Dimming the lights for a movie

Dimming the lights automatically when you start a movie is the obvious use for INSTEON. Thanks to devices like the IRLinc from SmartLabs, the ISY-99i/IR from Universal Devices, and the EZUIRT from SimpleHomeNet, it's easy to make your lighting respond to IR signals in harmony with your home theater system.

TURNING DOWN THE LIGHTS FOR A MOVIE

WHAT YOU NEED

⇒ IRLinc (Instructions for EZUIRT are similar, ISY-99/IR can also perform this function).

WHAT TO DO

⇒ Plug the IRLinc into an outlet near your television, and route the IR Receiver to an area near your television. Using the double-sided tape, mount the receiver next to your television in an inconspicuous place.

⇒ Program your universal remote to mimic an NEC remote control.

⇒ Using the instructions that come with the IRLinc, link all the lights in your living room area to the IRLinc, and configure your universal remote to shut off the lights when you enable a movie scene.

Ventilating your A/V cabinet

Dimming the lights isn't the only think you can do with INSTEON. Nearly everyone who builds a complicated Audio Visual system decides they need to hide all the blinking lights in a cabinet or closet. The problem with hiding A/V components is that many of them generate considerable heat. Worse, those with hard disk drives, such as Tivos, DVRs, AppleTVs, or computers will suffer early death because of the heat they generate. You must ventilate an enclosed A/V cabinet, and INSTEON can help.

To correctly ventilate, you can't simply put a fan inside the cabinet. You need to exchange the hot air inside the cabinet with ambient air and ensure that air flows past all of the heat generating components. I recommend using low wattage 4" computer fans to move air past each hot component and one to pull air into the cabinet. By pulling air in, you can put a 4" filter on the inbound fan to trap dust. If you reverse the flow to pull air out of the cabinet, you create low pressure inside the cabinet and cause air to be pulled in through all the nooks and crannies and cannot control dust, which will wind up being pulled through your components leaving them coated in dust.

I'm going to recommend using A/C fans because they are powerful, even though they are noisy. Use a LampLinc to reduce the voltage to the fans to the point where they no longer make noise. Adjust the dim level until the resonant "buzz" caused by driving an inductive load is minimal, which indicates that the fan rotation is sympathetic with the duty cycle produced by the LampLinc. You can silence the fans by mounting them with foam so that the fans do not directly contact a hard surface.

You could also perform the same ventilation with 4" DC fans, using either an EZIO capable of driving low wattage DC loads or a 12-volt transformer and a LampLinc Relay.

VENTILATE AN A/V CABINET

WHAT YOU NEED

⇒ A number of 4" (120mm) A/C fans typified by Digi-Key part number 259-1389-ND, and a matching number of A/C power cords that you can connect to the fans using wire nuts.

⇒ A passive power splitter.

⇒ One LampLinc V2.

WHAT TO DO

⇒ Cut a 4" round hole in an appropriately hidden area of the A/V cabinet that vents to ambient air. You may need to get creative with 4" flexible dryer ducting to make this work.

⇒ Mount one of the fans and a matching filter to the vent hole such that the direction of airflow pushes air into the cabinet.

⇒ Place a fan next to each of the heat generating components such that it draws air out past the component's heat vents.

⇒ Plug each fan into a passive splitter, and plug the splitter into the LampLinc. Do not plug the LampLinc into a filtered splitter, as filters attenuate INSTEON signals.

⇒ Using HouseLinc or any other INSTEON dimmer controller, reduce the voltage to the fans until they are silent and the inductance buzz is minimized.

⇒ Link the LampLinc to your IRLinc to automatically turn the fans on and off with you're A/V components.

The Green Smart Home

A properly configured INSTEON smart home has the potential to cut your electricity usage—and bills—substantially by helping to eliminate the waste associated with lights left on in unoccupied spaces, by truly turning off sleeping appliances at night, and by reducing HVAC usage through smart management of fans and window closures.

> Remember that INSTEON systems do require power to operate, so you will have to save a moderate amount of power in order to achieve a "net positive" energy savings. Reducing A/C usage, heavy use of timers, and "all off" paths to make sure lights are not left on is the easiest way to accomplish significant energy savings.

Turning off lights

INSTEON is the perfect solution for people who want to make sure that they're minimizing their power draw for lighting. From a wide array of timer-based lights to the ability to integrate motion sensors with lighting, INSTEON allows you to minimize power draw throughout your home easily and with minimal inconvenience.

One of the best "Green features" of INSTEON is the ability of INSTEON dimmers to be programmed to come on at a level less than 100%—so you can set lamps and installed incandescent lights to draw less power every time you turn them on, and still bring the lights up further when you need to. This won't work for compact florescent lights, which must be switched from INSTEON relays.

Save Power by Dimming Lights By Default

⇒ INSTEON dimmers of all types can be programmed to come on by default to a lower level than 100%. Once you have your INSTEON dimmers installed, bring down the lights to a level that your comfortable with, and then program the dimmers to come on to that level rather than to 100%. You'll save energy and extend the life of your bulbs without having to think about it twice. Chapter 7 explains how to set default dim levels manually, and Chapter 8 describes how to do it with HouseLinc.

While traditional timer and occupancy sensors work well for situations such as utility rooms and bathrooms that are not normally occupied, INSTEON makes it easy to control lighting in rooms that are normally occupied. And INSTEON timers are more controllable than typical timers as well, and can be used to control more than just a single device.

Control All Lights and Fans From a Single Timer

What You Need

⇒ An INSTEON SwitchLinc Dimmer (#2476D) wired to your bathroom mirror or accessory lights.

⇒ An INSTEON SwitchLinc Relay (#2476S) wired to your bathroom Fan.

⇒ An INSTEON count-down timer such as the 8-button Keypad Count-down timer with dimmer (#2484DWH8) wired to your bathroom's primary light.

What To Do

⇒ Link the INSTEON Count-down timer to also control the SwitchLinc Relay connected to the fan, and both devices will go off when the countdown timer shuts off.

If you use HouseLinc software with a PLM to control INSTEON devices with your computer, the PLM can be programmed with events that will automatically trigger based on the time of day. You can use this feature to create an event at night to go through and turn off all your INSTEON devices. I set mine for midnight, but you can use whatever time it is that everyone will be asleep. This makes sure that no lights or appliances are left on over night.

The use of HouseLinc is covered in Chapter 8.

Turning off "leaky" appliances

Some devices that automatically turn off or enter a "sleep" mode actually still use quite a bit of power. You can determine exactly how much by plugging a power leakage monitor between the outlet and the device's plug. Home Theater equipment is especially notorious for this behavior because this type of equipment has to stay on to watch for remote control codes.

Kitchen appliances such as coffee makers, microwave ovens and devices that use power adapters or battery chargers also continuously draw current and are good candidates for being turned off when not in use. Your microwave will constantly blink "12:00" if you turn it off routinely, but that's a small price to pay for the energy savings and you probably don't rely on it for the time anyway.

You can avoid inconvenience by using an Insteon timer or a PLM event to turn appliances off at night, say from 10:00 p.m. to 6:00 a.m. By the time you're awake in the morning, your devices will be powered back up and ready for you without wasting energy through the night.

Your home network may also be a candidate for shutting off at night. When you add up your cable modem, router, switches, and wireless access points, you'll reach 200 watts pretty quickly. Turning them off at night not only saves power, but also secures your computers and wireless access points—if they can't be reached, they can't be hacked. This won't work if you download content over night routinely, or if you have network security cameras.

For A/V equipment, use an ApplianceLinc before the power-strip that you connect your devices to. By linking the ApplianceLinc to an Insteon IRLinc, you can have the equipment come on simultaneously when the IRLinc senses a remote in use. Use another "always-on" power-strip for devices that must remain on overnight, such as TiVo. This way, you can make your decision about whether any particular device should be shut off by simply plugging it into the appropriate power strip.

There are a couple of real-world caveats to this type of use however:

- Insteon devices do draw power, albeit a small amount. An ApplianceLinc draws 6w of power continuously, which may be similar to what a sleeping device draws. Use a plug-in "through outlet" power meter to decide whether you're really saving a significant amount of power.
- Some devices may change to a default mode of operation after being turned on that isn't what you expect or want. If it's problematic, you'll have to leave these devices on.
- Digital Video Recorders (DVR, such as a TiVo) must be left on in order to record shows when you aren't using your system. Also, computer-based devices containing hard disk drive storage (such as an Apple TV) should be shut down rather than having power cut to them.
- Your devices will miss the first remote control code that triggers their power up because they were off when it happened, and it may take most devices a few seconds to come fully on-line. Your universal remote will have to be programmed with a delay to account for cold-start times.
- Devices can draw significantly more power while starting up than when in standby, so you probably don't want to be turning them on and off many times throughout the day.

AUTOMATICALLY POWERING OFF LEAKY DEVICES AT NIGHT, WITH MANUAL OVERRIDE

WHAT YOU NEED

⇒ An ApplianceLinc for each group of appliances on a power strip that you want to control as a group.

⇒ Any Insteon controller such as a ControlLinc, RemoteLinc, or IRLinc to trigger the devices to turn on. For Microwave ovens and coffee makers, consider linking them to a KeypadLinc button on a kitchen main switch.

⇒ Any INSTEON device with an integrated time-of-day timer, such as the INSTEON Powerline Controller (#2414U) and a computer running HouseLinc (#2416D) or the SimpleHomeNet EZServe (31279).

WHAT TO DO

⇒ Link the ApplianceLinc to the selected manual controller or to an INSTEON switch.

⇒ Create a Time-of-day event in the home automation controller to power off the ApplianceLincs at Midnight every day. Do not create an automatic event to power them back on.

⇒ Manually turn on the devices whenever you want to use them. Getting into the habit of simply turning them on when you want to use them saves considerably more power than automatically turning them back on when you are home.

Environmental control

INSTEON can help you manage the HVAC systems in your home to use good weather when it's available rather than simply having the HVAC system running constantly.

By using vent fans that communicate to move air throughout the house, and by using casement windows that can be opened or closed based on the inside and outside temperature, the weather, and the occupancy of the home, you can minimize your use of heating and air conditioning systems to keep your home comfortable.

The major climate control problem that we have in my house is that we usually don't need A/C—the weather is generally cooler than 78 degrees, so we just leave the windows open and set the A/C not to come on below 78 degrees. The problem is that when it does get hot outside, the inside air will go above 78 and the A/C will come on—with the windows open. This just wastes power.

The solution was to interrupt the A/C compressor with a 30-amp INSTEON 220V switch and to link it to a button on a KeypadLinc near the windows. Now we can easily and directly control whether the A/C will come on or not once we've closed the windows.

Manual A/C Control

What You Need

⇒ One KeypadLinc or other INSTEON controller
⇒ One EZSwitch30 220VAC switch

What To Do

⇒ Install the EZSwitch 220VAC switch on your A/C compressor.
⇒ Link the EZSwitch to a button on the KeypadLinc controller. Turn the button on to allow the A/C to run, and off to disable it based on whether or not your windows are opened.

INSTEON compatible thermostats are an easy way to enable your thermostat to be controllable from anywhere in the house. Link it to a switch by your nightstand to lower the heat for the night or to an exit button by each door to turn off the HVAC system when you're not at home.

Controlling the thermostat

What You Need

⇒ One INSTEON Remote Control Thermostat (#2491T1)
⇒ One INSTEON Access Point if you don't already have one

What To Do

⇒ Attach the INSTEON Remote Control Thermostat interface to your existing thermostat.

⇒ Set the thermostat to the mode and temperature that you want to associate with an INSTEON controller.

⇒ Set the INSTEON controller to SET mode.

⇒ Return to the thermostat and press the SET button on the side of the thermostat for six seconds. The thermostat will now go to this mode and temperature when you press the ON button for the INSTEON controller. OFF commands are ignored.

⇒ Repeat this sequence for each controller/temperature setting you want to make.

Garage Door Control

There are numerous ways to control your garage door using INSTEON technology. From opening the door itself to triggering lights when the door opens to remotely closing your garage door over the Internet, INSTEON can make coming home really easy.

> Never remotely close your garage door unless you can be certain that it is safe to do so. Ensure that you have beam-breaker interlocks working at that the garage door will stop at a safe pressure.

Detecting Garage Door opening

The earliest easy signal you can provide when you're arriving home is the signal you send from the garage door opener in your car. There are numerous ways to detect garage door opening and trigger an INSTEON response:

- With a garage door signal receiver and an I/O Linc
- With an EZX-10RF and your HomeLink compatible car
- With a door contact closure sensor and an I/OLinc
- With a wireless door contact sensor and an Access Point
- With an INSTEON compatible motion sensor

For the best reliability, security, and lowest cost you'll want to avoid wireless signals completely and use a simple garage door contact closure and an I/OLinc plugged into a nearby outlet.

DETECT GARAGE DOOR OPENING

WHAT YOU NEED
⇒ One garage door contact closure
⇒ One I/OLink. Smarthome.com sells a garage door closure sensor kit with all required parts.

WHAT TO DO
⇒ Mount the garage door contact closure at the base of your garage door. You probably already have on to detect the garage door at bottom, so be sure to mount the new one on the other side.
⇒ Wire the garage door contact closure to the I/OLinc.
⇒ Plug the I/OLinc into a nearby outlet and link it to your garage lights. Now your garage installed lighting will come on when you raise your garage door.

You can also wire an I/OLinc to your garage door directly to close it based on an INSTEON command if your garage door has an isolated input to cause closure (most do). In many cases you could also open the garage door this way. Be exceptionally careful about remotely operating a garage door however—if you can't see it, you can't be certain that it can be safely operated.

Closing the Garage Door

The other half of garage door control is ensuring that it's closed, especially in case you've left the house and think you may have forgotten to close it.

In order to close your garage door when you aren't home, you have to be able to remotely access your INSTEON network:
• Via the web using a SmartLinc, EZSrve, or ISY-99
• Via telephone dial-in control using an ELK-M1 Gold

Given that you've got a way to remotely signal any INSTEON device, you then have three options to remotely close your garage door:
• The Smarthome I/O Link Garage Door Kit, which contains an I/O Link and all the equipment necessary to both indicate your garage-door status and remotely open or close it.

- The GarageHawk, which is specifically designed to close a garage door with no possibility of accidentally opening it.
- An EZIO output wired to your garage door opener to trigger a close. This option requires some Do-It-Yourself acumen. The EZIO8SA comes with instructions for configuring it to both detect door opening and close the door.

The first two options are relatively easy to setup and configure. The absolutely least expensive way to go to achieve remote closure of the garage door would be to combine the Smarthome I/O Link Garage Door Kit with a SmartLinc web controller, providing remote closure control for about $200.

Summary

The great strength of INSTEON is how easy and inexpensive it is to get started. Unlike most smart-home systems, you don't have to go all out and buy the system in advance of knowing how to use it (or even whether you'll use it). You can get started by solving very specific problems, certain in the knowledge that you can build your system piece-by-piece into an entire smart-home system.

This capacity for "organic" growth rather than front-loaded planning that most systems require is a great strength of INSTEON technology, because you simply cannot know exactly how you're going to use your system in advance.

Chapter 5
The INSTEON Smart-Home

Why do you want a smart home system?

The answer to that question will guide your planning for a whole home electrical remodel or new construction. If you are facing a rebuild or electrical remodel, you can save a considerable amount of money by installing an INSTEON system at the outset rather than wiring with traditional methods and then organically growing a system.

Keep in mind that you will not be able to predict all of your potential uses, so take a minimalistic approach in the beginning and be prepared for some organic change to your requirements and systems after you've moved in.

This chapter will walk you through a practical approach to INSTEON planning for the whole home by marking up a set of prints with codes that designate each device you'll need at the position that you will install it. As you go through the chapter, you'll be prompted to think through potential uses and make decisions about them, marking up your set of house plans as you go. At the end of the chapter, you can simply count the codes on the plans to produce your bill of materials for ordering, and you'll have your plans ready to go for installation when your devices arrive.

Defining Your Goals

Our home automation system started with these two simple goals:

- We wanted to be able to turn all the lights in the house off as we left the house or went to bed
- We wanted to be able to light a pathway to the kid's bedrooms from the car when we arrived home, for the frequent case when we'd arrive home at night and have to carry them to bed because they fell asleep in the car.

From these two simply stated goals, all of our design choices sprang. If one of your requirements is "turn all the lights off when I leave the home or go to bed" then you'll have to put an INSTEON switch on every light in your house.

Once we knew we were going to have a smart home system, we subsequently made some building decisions to save money and maintenance in the future.

Initial changes we made include:

- We eliminated all exterior light switches for our back patio and roof deck lighting, and replaced them with InLineLinc relays near the back door and a RemoteLinc that can be taken with us when we're outside. This is more convenient, less expensive, and maintenance free compared to exterior switches.
- We installed an INSTEON compatible security system. Instead of an annoying siren, the security system brings up the bedroom and living room lights when triggered. This makes false alarms less annoying, doesn't wake the kids, and provides immediate light if we do have to react to something (usually, one of the kids).
- We informed the electricians that no multi-way switches would be required—all installed lighting should be run to a single switch. This saved about 10% off the cost of the electrical contracting, which nearly paid for all the INSTEON devices.

- In our city, kitchen lights are required to be compact fluorescent lights that can't be dimmed. We have an array of twelve cans in the ceiling, and have them setup so that we can turn on 1, 3, 6, 9 or all 12 in a pattern to get the amount of light we want.

The system we have now can do much more than our original goals required, and after we moved in we found ourselves making little changes to the way lights function all over the house—little things that we did because we could and because they made the home more convenient that we never would have thought of prior to actually using the system.

Examples of changes we've made include:

- The wall switch next to my chair in the living room is linked to the bedroom lights and fans in the Kid's bedrooms. If they turn a light on to play when they're supposed to be in bed, I can just reach over from my chair in the living room and turn it back off.
- Our television remote control will automatically turn off the all the living room and kitchen lights when we start a movie.
- A long basement hallway was wired with the light-switch at the wrong-end, causing us to have to walk through the dark hallway to turn the light on. A simple matter of linking it to a switch near the correct end solved the problem.
- My son likes to have a particular plug in fan blowing on him as he falls asleep. Turning it off used to mean going into his room at night and finding the fan's cord switch in the dark. Now we have it plugged into an appliance link and linked to the ceiling fan switch on his wall so we can turn it off from the door.
- We installed a SmartLinc web controller that works reasonably well from my and my wife's cell phone web browsers—so we're always carrying a remote for lights on our person while we're in the house. It works well for those times when we've forgotten to take the RemoteLinc out to the patio or we want to turn the downstairs lights off.

I won't bore you with additional uses—the point is that we hadn't predicted any of these uses in advance. You'll find that you won't have predicted the most common ways you use your system in advance either.

Since most home construction costs are computed in terms of cost-per-square-foot, it's useful to compare the cost of INSTEON in terms of square feet. Typical homes have about ten light switches per thousand square feet. Multiplying that by fifty dollars per switch on average, and you can plan on INSTEON costing about 50¢ per square foot at the time this book was written for lighting control of an entire home. If you have requirements beyond lighting or want to get fancy with home automation and control, you'll get nearer to $1 per square foot. In my home, I wound up at about 85¢ per square foot (excluding the security system that we would have installed irrespective of the Smarthome installation).

Remodeling For INSTEON

INSTEON doesn't require you to open walls or incorporate major equipment to install it in a typical home—simply turning off your circuit breaker and replacing switches is all that is required in many cases.

There are a couple of things you will need to change, however:
- Check for neutrals in switchboxes and determine how to proceed
- Convert existing multi-way switches to typical switches.

Check older homes for neutrals

If your home is more than twenty years old, you need to open a few light switches and ensure that you have neutrals wired to the switch junction boxes before you begin ordering equipment. Check for proper grounding wires while you're at it.

If your home is wired without neutrals in switchboxes, you will need to decide how to proceed:
- You can upgrade your electrical wiring to comply with modern code
- You can use INSTEON Two-wire switches

Upgrading your electrical wiring

If you choose to upgrade your electrical wiring, and it's highly likely you'll need an electrician to perform the upgrade, and that the electrician will want to open up walls to accomplish the work. In this case, you should be prepared for a substantial remodeling cost and combine the electrical remodel with other remodeling work.

Using Two-wire INSTEON switches

If you do not have neutrals wired to switches, you may want to order 2-wire INSTEON switches rather than upgrading your wiring.

Two-wire INSTEON switches work by placing the relay or dimmer module that controls the light at the fixture in the ceiling where neutral and hot exist, rather than in the switch Junction box. The runner to the switch junction box is then connected to a special switch plate that is powered by the dimmer/relay module.

This technique eliminates the need to use three-wire switches, but it is more complicated to install because it requires opening up each electrical fixture to place a module behind it. It is considerably less expensive than upgrading your electrical wiring, however.

Bear in mind that not all types and colors of INSTEON switches are available in two-wire configurations.

WHAT YOU NEED: ADD INSTEON CONTROL TO A TWO-WIRE SWITCH

⇒ One INSTEON 2-Wire dimmer (#2474D) or on/off switch (#2474S) kit for each two-wire switch you want to add to your INSTEON system

Rewiring Multi-way switches

Multi-way switching works differently in INSTEON than in traditional electrical wiring. For a fixture with multiple switch locations, you will need to determine which switch you want to use as the "primary switch" for the fixture when you convert to INSTEON.

You then have three options for each of the remaining switches:

- Replace them with INSTEON switches that have no wired load and which are linked back to the primary load switch to match your current functionality.
- Plate them over if the switch location isn't needed.
- Convert them to outlets.

You cannot leave them wired as multi-way switches because that will interrupt power delivery to the other INSTEON switches in the multi-way circuit.

Building for INSTEON

If you are building a new home, you can save yourself some money and effort by eliminating the wiring of multi-way switches. Depending on the size and complexity of your installation, you may save enough in simplified runs and lower labor costs to pay for the cost of your INSTEON switches.

> Tell the electricians to wire the home with a single switch per fixture (no multi-way switching), from switch to fixture.

Wiring in a switch-fixture pattern will allow you to use two-wire romex cable throughout. If you wire fixture-switch, you will have to use three-wire romex cable from the fixture to the switch.

You can also eliminate exterior switches for patio lighting and deck lighting. Exterior switches are subject to a lot more weather related corrosion and fail earlier than interior switches even when they are enclosed in proper weatherproof enclosures. Wire switches for exterior fixtures to the interior of the home in convenient locations such as near backdoors or in utility rooms, and then use Access Points and a RemoteLinc to control them when you're outside.

Have electricians leave a breaker slot open so you can have a hardwired phase coupler installed at the panel. Better yet, hand them a hard-wired phase bridge and have them install it.

INSTEON Switch Types

In this book, I use the term "SwitchLinc" to refer to "any INSTEON controlled switch." In practice, you'll need to determine exactly which INSTEON switch you will use at each location.

The criteria are:

- The load type (on/off relay, 600w dimmer)
- The switch type (paddle, toggle, keypad, or none)
- The installation type (plug-in or wired-in)
- Color

You can use table 5.1 to quickly identify which switch you want based on these criteria.

Type	Wired On/Off	Wired Dimmer	Similar plug-in option
Paddle	SwitchLinc Relay	SwitchLinc Dimmer	ControlLinc
Toggle	ToggleLinc Relay	ToggleLinc Dimmer	ControlLinc
Keypad	KeypadLink Relay	KeypadLinc Dimmer	KeypadLinc Tabletop
Low cost	ICON Relay	ICON Dimmer	ControlLinc
Outlet	OutletLinc	LampLinc (plug-in)	ApplianceLinc
Timer	SwitchLinc Timer	(none)	TimerLinc
Hidden	InLineLinc Relay	InLineLinc Dimmer	ApplianceLinc

Table 5.1: INSTEON switch selector

Chapter 10 details INSTEON switches and other devices.

Determining the load type for switches

Most INSTEON devices come in two types based on the load they control:

- On/Off non-dimming Relay switches
- Dimmer switches

All electrical appliances and lights can be controlled by relays. A dimmer can control only incandescent lights.

If you don't know what the load type is or the load type may change, use a relay.

Relays

Switches for typical on/off switched loads use the term "Relay" or "ON/OFF" in their name to refer to the electrical component that actually causes the switching: A relay.

Relays are on/off devices that can be used to control any device. They use the same mechanism as an ApplianceLinc. You must use relays on fluorescent and fan loads because the way dimmers rapidly switch the electrical power interferes with their operation. They're safe to use everywhere, but they can't be dimmed. Relays can also provide more power to the load than a typical dimmer.

If the switch controls fluorescent lighting or a fan, you should use a SwitchLinc Relay.

Relay devices typically have the term "Relay" in their name, such as the "SwitchLinc Relay." The exception to this is the ApplianceLinc, which is also a relay-based device.

Dimmers

Switches for dimmable loads use the term dimmer in their name. Dimmers rapidly switch the electrical load to reduce the amount of power that reaches the device. Incandescent lights use less power and become dimmer when this happens—but dimmers can only be used on incandescent loads.

Putting a dimmer on other types of loads can cause the dimmer or the load device to rapidly wear out or make a noticeable humming noise. Don't put a dimmer on fluorescent lights unless the lights specifically state that they work with electronic dimmers. INSTEON (and my electrician) both state that dimmers should not be used on ceiling fans because the rapid electronic switching method used by the dimmer to reduce power can cause the fan to buzz. I've done it anyway, and while it does work, the hum is quite noticeable at certain speeds and unnoticeable at others.

Typical fan controls look almost exactly like typical dimmers, but they operate completely differently. Fan controls are variable resisters that dissipate excess power as heat, whereas lighting dimmers are semiconductor high-speed switches that are much more efficient and do not heat up. There are no INSTEON fan controllers made as of the publication date of this book.

INSTEON says that its electronic dimmers can drive magnetic transformers for low-voltage lighting. I've wired one up and while it works just fine, the dimmer does make a slight buzzing sound that I don't hear on typical incandescent loads.

Typical INSTEON dimmers can handle up to 600-watt loads. INSTEON makes a more robust dimmer that can handle up to 1000-watt loads, but it costs a bit more.

When you perform power calculations for dimmers, remember to add up the values of all the light bulbs that the switch operates. For example, If you have four recessed lights in the living room that are dimmed by a single switch, add the wattage of all four lights to determine the total wattage for the dimmer. Be sure to drive no more than 75% of the rated load to be safe in case higher wattage lights are installed in the future as well. Finally, the National Electric Code requires that you do not go over 80% of the rated load if more than one dimmer is installed in the same junction box.

For example, I have a chandelier with 12 lights, each using a 40W light bulb. This totals 600W. If I used a 600W dimmer, there would be no margin at all, and would be illegal to install in a junction box with another dimmer. The solution is to use a dimmer rated for 1000W.

INSTEON devices that control incandescent loads usually use the term "Dimmer" in their name, such as the ToggleLinc Dimmer. The exception is the LampLinc, which is the dimming version of an ApplianceLinc.

Determining the key type for switches

Most of the switches in your home will be replaced by SwitchLinc or ToggleLinc single-switch devices. But at major entryways and high-use locations, consider using KeypadLinc switches so that you can enable path and scene lighting easily.

It's not always easy to tell where you're going to want to put KeypadLincs—but you can always swap them around after the fact if you find you're not using them in a certain location.

In my home, we have KeypadLinc switches in the following locations:
- In the entryway at the front door and garage door.
- In the garage
- At the top of the stairs to the second floor
- At the back door
- In the master bedroom
- On the wall next to my chair in the living room
- At the end of a hallway whose actual switch is at the other end

Of these locations, we predicted the first four correctly, but the second three came after-the-fact when we were in the home and realized we wanted more control from specific areas or where we had a problem to remediate.

In general, you can figure that 10% to 20% of your switches will be KeypadLincs and the remainder will be either SwitchLincs or ToggleLincs.

SwitchLinc and ToggleLinc

SwitchLinc and ToggleLinc switches are direct replacements for a typical solitary light switch. SwitchLincs are Decora style paddle switches, and ToggleLincs are traditional toggle switch style switches. Otherwise they are the same.

Use SwitchLinc or ToggleLinc switches to control a single light or appliance Load.

KeypadLinc

KeypadLinc switches can be configured as six or eight button single-gang keypads—they're actually the same device but come with two different keypad overlays and are configured in software to work in six or eight button modes.

In six-button mode, the upper large On button and the lower large Off button control the primary load, and the four center buttons only send INSTEON signals to other devices.

In Eight button mode, the "A" or top-left button is a toggle button that controls the primary load, and the remaining seven buttons only send INSTEON signals to other devices.

Use a KeypadLinc in six-button mode to replace a switch in your house and add buttons to control other individual devices. This is a great way to put other controllers of a particular light or device at an entryway to a room for example, without making it difficult to determine which buttons take the function of the original switch.

Use a KeypadLinc in eight-button mode as a main control panel for lighting scenes and paths at major entryways such as the front and back door, and in places where you naturally want the ability to control a number of devices because you spend a lot of time there. For example, you might put one in a master bedroom, at the front and back doors, and in the garage.

> Put a plug-in KeypadLinc Tabletop on your nightstand in your bedroom for a simple, small, and inconspicuous way to turn lights off when you go to bed and turn them on when you wake up.

Laser etched KeypadLinc buttons

Smarthome offers laser-etched buttons for both KeypadLincs. They're very well made and look great—they put a very elegant finishing touch on your switches.

But don't order them in advance of moving in if you're building a home new construction. When we planned our house, we planned where we would put the KeypadLincs and defined what we thought would make good lighting paths. But small changes to the house electrical layout occurred after we made our order, and once we moved in, we found that we didn't use everything the way we thought we were going to in advance. The way we referred to rooms changed after we moved in as well. KeypadLincs were also moved around, from locations where a simple switch was all that was necessary to locations where we discovered that we wanted more control.

The end result was that about 50% of our pre-planned keys are now completely obsolete and had to be replaced. Save yourself the planning and waste by ordering your etched buttons once your system has settled.

> Use a post-it note above your KeypadLincs prior to ordering etched keys to keep track of their purpose. You can re-write them frequently as your programming changes, and then order your etched keys once your system has settled.

InLineLinc

InLineLinc switches are responders without buttons on them—they are designed to be linked to another INSTEON switch to be controlled and either hidden in the wall or ceiling or plated over if they replace a switch.

Use InLineLinc switches to eliminate hard-to-reach switches, and to add control to individual lights in the ceiling at the light fixture. For example, you can use InLineLinc relays to add individual control to lights that have been placed on the same circuit and are controlled together, such as a line of ceiling cans, or to put switched control on an outlet inside the wall.

Once linked, you rarely need to see or update an InLineLinc device again, so you can feel free to put them inside walls and ceilings. The only time I've needed to un-plate them was to link them to an INSTEON SmartLinc network controller.

TimerLinc

TimerLincs are regular SwitchLinc and KeypadLinc hardware but with different firmware that gives them the capability to automatically turn off after a period of time. Use TimerLincs to control devices that shouldn't remain on for long after a person leaves a room, such as on bathroom lights and fans, closet and attic lights, hallway lights, garages, laundry rooms, and anywhere else that lights are routinely "left on" because the room isn't typically occupied.

INSTEON Planning

If you are performing a whole-house electrical remodel or building new construction, you can save yourself both hassle and over-purchasing by performing some up-front planning.

Use your electrical system blueprints as a basis for INSTEON planning. These prints will show the locations of all the switches in your home. If you don't have a set, use a 2D layout program such as Visio, ConceptDraw, or OmniGraffle to create a rough map of your home and all the current switch locations. Draw a line from the switch locations to the fixture that they control as shown in figure 5.x below.

INITIAL WHOLE-HOUSE SWITCH LAYOUT

⇒ On your plans, place a switch symbol ($) at each switch location. Draw a curved arc to the fixture controlled by each switch.

⇒ Once you've laid out your switches and fixtures, mark each fixture type as "L" for incandescent light, "S" for Relay controlled florescent, "F" for inductive load fans, "V" for low-voltage, and "A" for a switch that controls an appliance outlet.

⇒ Mark each switch location with a "KL" for KeypadLinc if it is near a major entryway, or "SL" for SwitchLinc otherwise. Suffix them with a "D" for Dimmer if the connected fixture load type is "L" Incandescent, or with "R" For On/Off Relay otherwise.

⇒ For lamps and other plug-in appliances that you wish to control, mark the location of the outlet with "AL" for ApplianceLinc or "LL" for LampLinc as appropriate.

Keep your plans handy as you proceed through the remainder of this chapter. When you've finished, you'll have a complete count of all the devices you need to purchase to create your system.

> It's easy to tell where you should use KeypadLincs—
> Anywhere you currently have a gang of more than
> two switches is an ideal location.

Make choices that allow you to defer as many of the system devices as possible. This way, you'll have a basic system up and running and will have learned how you will use the system before you spend a lot of money on esoteric devices that you may find you don't need.

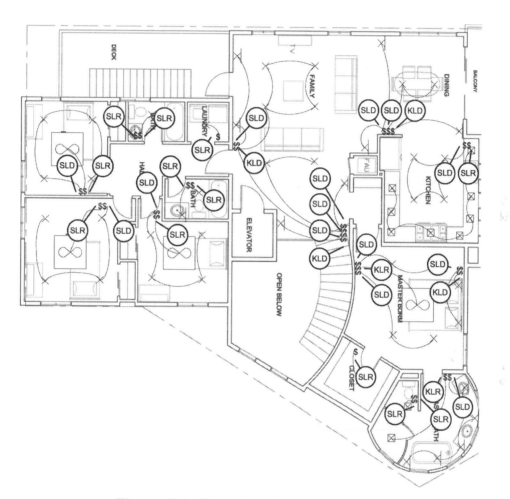

Figure 5.1: Electrical Switch Layouts

Upfront Decisions

There are only a few basic decisions you need to make when you plan your INSTEON system:

- What type of phase bridge will you use?
- What type of central home automation controller, if any, will you use?
- Will you integrate INSTEON with your home security system?
- Will you integrate INSTEON with your environmental controls?

The next few sections cover these decisions in detail.

What type of phase bridge will you use?

If you are building or remodeling, you should definitely install a hard-wired phase bridge. Using Access Points to phase bridges is more expensive, more visible, and slightly less reliable than using a hard-wired bridge.

The choice then is quite simple:

- If you are installing or remodeling your electrical panel, have the electricians install a hard-wired phase bridge.
- If your electrical panel will remain the same during your remodel or installation, use a plug-in 220V phase bridge.
- If you don't have an available 220V outlet, you rent, or you want a non-permanent installation, use Access Points

That's all there is to it.

DECISION POINT: PHASE BRIDGE

⇒ Mark "HPB" next to the electrical panel for "Hardwired Phase Bridge," "PPB" next to a 220V outlet for "Plug-in Phase Bridge," or "AP" next to two circuits on the different phases of your home.

What type of home automation controller, if any, will you use?

The question of central home automation control can be complicated. Firstly, INSTEON doesn't require central control of any kind—it works perfectly well as a peer-to-peer solution without any central controller (unlike just about every other smart home available). But central controllers can be convenient, and for large installations having the ability to centrally program the system is nearly a necessity.

The complexity of your link maps increases exponentially with the number of devices that you have. For a few devices, manually creating and deleting links is no big deal. But every time you add a device and link it others, it becomes less and less likely that you'll be able to keep track of all those links. You'll start factory-resetting devices because you can't figure out why they're behaving the way they are, and re-linking from scratch.

There are two ways that home automation controllers work:
- By programming the links you make into the INSTEON hardware directly, so that the home automation controller need not be running in order for your scenes and paths to work
- By maintaining the links and directly controlling devices, so that INSTEON links are not used and the home automation controller must be running in order to control devices.

Of the two methods, the first is both more difficult and more robust: It takes time to determine what links exist and to push them out to INSTEON devices as well as good programming in order for a home automation controller to determine what links ought to be programmed, but because the home automation controller needn't be running, your INSTEON system will be more reliable. You should prefer home automation controllers that correctly create INSTEON links over those that merely directly control devices.

HouseLinc

If you have more than about twenty INSTEON devices, the complexity of managing and changing links will become a disincentive to using the system. All installations of this size or larger should be managed using HouseLinc or another home automation controller that can program links back into devices.

HouseLinc (or an equivalent option such as Indigo 4 or the ISY-99) is a necessary component of any large INSTEON system in my opinion. Although it does have a learning curve, it keeps the complexity of changing links manageable. I don't know how I would get along without it.

> HouseLinc is by far the simplest and least expensive central management system for INSTEON. I strongly recommend using it for whole-house INSTEON deployments.

HouseLinc 2 is the current version at the time this book went to press. HouseLinc 2 differs from HouseLinc 1 primarily in that it uploads timer and scene control to the Powerline Controller so the program need not be left running.

Keep in mind that most 3rd party home automation controllers can directly control INSTEON devices but they cannot program links into the devices. If the home automation controller fails, so does all of your automation. You will have a much more reliable system if you use a home automation controller that can program links back into the devices and does not rely on direct control except for event management.

> The ISY-99i is just as good as HouseLinc at managing links, although the user interface is more complicated.

DECISION POINT: HOUSELINC

⇒ If you are going to use HouseLinc, mark "PLM" on your plans near an outlet next to the computer that you will install the software on.

HouseLinc isn't marketed as a remote control solution. But if you've got a couple of computers in your home, it can be used as such. HouseLinc has the flexibility to control any INSTEON device in the house, which means that you can use it to do things on a whim that you haven't planned in advance—and quite a tool for discovering what you do want to be able to do. For example, my kids were in the habit of turning their lights back on and playing in their bedrooms after bedtime, which I was able to put an end to by simply turning their lights back off whenever they came on. This wasn't in my original planning, but it revealed a very typical use case that I subsequently programmed into my web-based controller.

HouseLinc is detailed in Chapter 8.

Simple Web Controllers

Web browsers are becoming more common all the time. If you have a Windows Mobile, Palm Treo, Apple iPhone or similar "full web" smart phone on your person most of the time and you already have a network in your home, a web-based controller will turn it into an easy-to-use remote control for you. Be sure that you're taking all the occupants of your house into account, however. If you're the sort of person that has a web browser handy most of the time, a web-based controller may be your best solution.

The EZServe and a small mobile web browser such as an iPhone or iPod Touch makes a very flexible remote control solution, although it is quite a bit more expensive than a RemoteLinc unless you already happen to have one. You'll also need a WiFi network to connect the dots. The EZServe website is a bit clunky on smartphones, however.

The SmartLinc is quite similar to the EZServe with a user interface designed specifically for smartphones, and is less expensive.

You needn't purchase a web-controller up-front. They are easy to add to your system at any time.

Carrying a remote on your person makes these simple web controllers far more useful in my opinion than sophisticated home automation controllers. But if you don't have remotes on your person or within easy reach, you'll rarely if ever use this type of controller.

> Many home automation controllers, including the ISY-99i, also provide web interfaces for use from mobile devices.

DECISION POINT: WEB BASED CONTROLLER

⇒ If you will be purchasing a web-based controller up-front, mark "WEB" on your plans next to the location of your wireless base station or cable/DSL router that the device will plug into.

Home Automation Controllers

Choose a home automation controller when you have multiple home automation systems to bridge between (such as Z-Wave and INSTEON) or when you want to integrate multimedia systems such as ambient music or home theater in complex ways. Home automation controllers interface with the INSTEON system using either a serial or USB PowerLinc power-line controller.

> If you have decided to use a home automation controller, you should select it up front and use it to program your system rather than manually creating links.

Keep in mind however that sophisticated home automation controllers create a single point of failure in your system. They are very expensive, and they don't make the programming or configuration of your system any easier than a good link manager like HouseLinc. The core problem is that making good definitions of what you want to have happen is difficult, and while home automation controllers can technically do anything you want, they cannot make intelligent decisions about how to react to numerous inputs to create a response that is always appropriate. And when the response isn't appropriate, you're going to be confused about why strange events are occurring.

> If you are leaning towards a home automation controller, check out the ISY-99i from Universal Devices first. It works well, is the only home automation controller designed specifically for INSTEON, is compatible with the widest array of INSTEON devices, and is remarkably inexpensive.

It is far simpler to tell your smart-home system what you want than to program it to figure it out. Choose simple command systems over predictive or "intelligent" systems that might be right 80% of the time and leave you annoyed 20% of the time.

I haven't met a person yet who has truly configured a home automation controller completely to the point where they (and their spouse) are happy with it.

DECISION POINT: HOME AUTOMATION CONTROLLER

⇒ If you will be using a home automation controller or a computer running home automation software, mark "PLM" on your plans near your wireless network hub or Cable/DSL Router where it will be installed.

Will you integrate INSTEON with your home security system?

You have four options when it comes to security and INSTEON:
- Don't integrate security.
- Use the Elk M1 Gold security system.
- Use SimpleHomeNet EZIO devices to integrate with an existing alarm system.
- Create a simple INSTEON security system from scratch using all INSTEON devices.

Non-integrated security

Do you need to link your security system with INSTEON? The primary reason for connecting the systems is to perform actions other than alarming on security events, such as automatically bringing up exterior lights or master bedroom lights when a security event occurs. This is a good reason to integrate a security system, but it's pretty much the only one. If this isn't what you intend to have happen, there's little reason to integrate your security system with INSTEON.

Integrating with Elk M1 Gold

If you intend to integrate INSTEON with your home security system and you are acquiring a system, you should look into the Elk M1 Gold security system. It is compatible with INSTEON, meaning that it can control INSTEON devices based on security events. However, INSTEON devices cannot control the security system. You can program lights to come up when security systems trigger using this system.

To be frank, however, the INSTEON compatibility is rather "tacked on" and not very simple to accomplish. Security systems can be difficult to program and configure, and there are a number of firmware updates you'll have to do to get the security system configured correctly for INSTEON. When completed, it does work well and you can configure the security keypads to control INSTEON paths, eliminating the need for a KeypadLinc anywhere that you have an Elk security keypad. It's much easier to simply use a KeypadLinc in my opinion.

Specifics on how to integrate Elk M1 Gold with INSTEON are provided in Chapter 9.

DECISION POINT: ELK M1 GOLD SECURITY SYSTEM

$\Rightarrow$ If you will be installing an Elk M1 Gold, mark "ELK" on your plans in the location where you will put the security panel, and mark "ESK" on your plans where you will put Elk Security Keypads.

Integrating Security with SimpleHomeNet EZIO

If you won't be replacing your security system, you can use SimpleHomeNet EZIO controllers to integrate both inputs and outputs on your alarm panel with I/O on the EZIO controllers. An output on an EZIO can be wired to an alarm sensor on the alarm panel to trigger an alarm, and an output on the panel can be wired to an EZIO input to trigger an event.

> You can integrate any security system with INSTEON using this technique, at any point in the future. Making this choice will allow you to defer integration until your INSTEON system is operational.

It is frankly probably easier to integrate your alarm panel using EZIO devices into an INSTEON system than it is to integrate it using the Elk M1 Gold system, and doing it this way keeps the two realms (security and home control) cleanly separated—you program only the EZIO device, not the security panel, for home automation requirements.

> Specifics on how to integrate security with EZIO devices are provided in Chapter 9.

DECISION POINT: ALARM PANEL INTEGRATION

⇒ If you will be integrating your existing security alarm panel with INSTEON using EZIO devices, mark "IO" next to the location of your alarm system panel.

Creating a simple security system using INSTEON devices

If your security needs are modest, it's cheaper and easier to create a simple home security system using all INSTEON devices.

Security systems at their heart are sense/react systems. INSTEON maps well to this pattern of behavior with its linked action/reaction model.

By establishing a set of sensors and a set of responders, you can easily create a security system ad-hoc.

There are three ways to create security sensors for INSTEON:

- Using the SimpleHomeNet EZSnsRF Dakota bridge for INSTEON. This device maps existing Dakota compatible sensors such as driveway/vehicle sensors, wireless motion detectors, and liquid level sensors.
- SimpleHomeNet EZIO devices can be used to integrate just about any typical wired sensor, such as window and door closures, motion detectors, glass breakage sensors, etc. With a large number of sensors (more than a dozen or so), it will be cheaper to use an inexpensive alarm system to handle the sensors and connect the alarm system alarm outputs to a single EZIO device.
- Use INSTEON Wireless motion sensor, wireless door closure sensor, and an INSTEON Access Point. This is the least expensive option over-all.

The other piece of the puzzle in an INSTEON only alarm system is the alarm outputs. This solution is simple: Simply plug an alarm light or AC siren into an ApplianceLinc, link it to the sensors, and it will go off whenever the sensors trip.

> You can create an INSTEON based security system at any time, and needn't plan for it in advance unless you want to. The security system should be the last phase of your INSTEON deployment if you do integrate it in the beginning.

⇒ Mark "MS" next to each area in your house where you will place a wireless motion sensor. Mark "SNS" at an outlet central to the motion sensors you've placed if you will be using EZSnsRF devices, or "AP" if you will be using INSTEON motion sensors. Bear in mind that Access Points only have an effective range of about 50 feet through indoor walls and you will likely need more than one. EZSnsRF devices should require only one receiver per home, as they are considerably longer range.

Will you integrate INSTEON with your environmental controls?

It is possible to integrate INSTEON with your environmental controls, to handle thermostat settings, casement window closure, irrigation, and ventilation.

Actually getting these systems to work well in an integrated fashion is a fairly expensive proposition, however, and it's generally less expensive to simply use a good controller designed for the problem.

What INSTEON could potentially provide is a way to schedule times when the home is typically unoccupied and a mechanism for the occupants to indicate that they are leaving or have arrived home. In these cases, INSTEON can provide energy savings by not running HVAC systems when nobody is home.

But that's really about all of the advantage that environmental control integration can provide at this point, and unless your home runs by a fairly regimented schedule or is typically unoccupied for long periods of time during the day, there's little advantage to be had by integrating INSTEON compatible environmental controls.

I recommend holding off on environmental controls until you've got your INSTEON system deployed and you know how you're using it. With a little forethought, you can plan for them now and integrate them later.

DECISION POINT: ENVIRONMENTAL CONTROLS

⇒ Mark "TS" next to each thermostat that you will be INSTEON enabling.

⇒ Mark "WC" at each casement window that you will be automating. Mark "IO" at some discreet outlet near the center of your Window closures.

Automatic Window Controllers

When it's a nice day outside, you should shut off your HVAC system and open the windows. But that's a lot of work to go to and quite frankly you may not even notice the weather outside—after all, nice weather is weather you don't notice.

Use an INSTEON compatible EZIO2x4 to keep track of inside and outside temperatures and wire the zone controls to the inputs of a motorized window controller for your modern casement windows. The EZIO2x4 has two analog inputs that can be wired to an interior and an exterior temperature sensor, or you can use a temp sensor that triggers inputs when high and low levels are met.

Wiring the outputs of the EZIO2x4 to the window closure controllers will trigger them to open or close when the temperature settings you establish have been met.

By linking it to an INSTEON compatible thermostat, another EZTherm2 that controls your HVAC system, or an EZSwitch30 connected to your HVAC compressor, you can shut off the HVAC while the windows are open. Finally, by linking the EZIO2x4 to an "exit" button on any INSTEON switch near your doors, you can shut the system off so that windows don't come open when you aren't occupying your home.

AUTOMATIC WINDOW CLOSURES

WHAT YOU NEED

⇒ One INSTEON controller such as a button on a KeypadLinc by each exit door in your home to indicate when you have exited your home. You could also link this system to an ELK security system to deactivate it when you arm the alarm system.

⇒ Two HAI in/out temp sensors (#110725) from www.smarthome.com

⇒ One SimpleHomeNet EZIO2x4 from www.simplehomenet.com to monitor temperatures and send control signals to your automatic windows.

⇒ A Wintrol LC-II Control Switch from www.wintrol.com for each set of up to three windows that you want to control as a group.

⇒ A Wintrol M2100 motor to match your casement windows from www.wintrol.com for each window you want to automatically control.

WHAT TO DO

⇒ Wire the HAI temperature sensors to the inputs of the EZIO2x4 I/O controller.

⇒ Wire the Wintrol LC-II switch to the outputs of the EZIO 2x4 controller.

⇒ Configure the EZIO2x4 to trigger a "close" event when the temperature goes below 68F degrees or above 80F

⇒ Configure the EZIO2x4 to trigger an "open" event when the temperature is between 70F and 78F.

WARNING: THIS PROCEDURE IS UNTESTED AND SHOULD BE CONSIDERED GUIDANCE ONLY

Living Room

The primary uses for INSTEON in the living room are integrating lighting with home theater, bringing down all the lights and lamps as a group, and establishing path lighting through the living room. Replacing each light switch in the living room with a SwitchLinc and plugging each lamp into a LampLinc module easily accomplishes all of these scenarios. You have a number of options for controlling the lighting once you have INSTEON switches throughout. If you've gone through your electrical layouts and replaced fixed switches with INSTEON switches already, you've covered most of the requirements for your living room.

Remotely controlling lights

Dimming or turning off lights without getting up turns out to be the use case we use most often in my home. There are a lot of ways to accomplish this task with INSTEON switches:

- With entertainment system universal remote and an IRLinc
- With a RemoteLinc and an Access Point
- Using a laptop and control software such as HouseLinc (this is only convenient if you happen to be using the computer already)
- Using any smartphone web browser and a web-based controller such as the SimpleHomeNet EZServe, the Universal Devices controller, or the SmartLinc Network controller.

Which method you choose depends on how you—and your family—intend to use the system. All of these methods cost less than $200, so it's certainly possible to use more than one.

SmartLinc

SmartLinc is a simple web based controller specifically designed to look good on the Apple iTouch, iPhone, and other small devices. It is by far the most convenient, most universal, and simplest to configure of all the remote control methods I've tried. We use it routinely in our house for just about all of our remote control needs.

> The best thing about the SmartLinc is that it allows me
> to use something I already have on my person—my
> cell phone—as a universal remote for my lighting.

The only downside of the SmartLinc is the cost: The controller itself is inexpensive (especially considering what competing functionality costs) but you must have a WiFi network in your house and the devices you'll need to control it with are expensive: iPod Touch, the least expensive web tablet you can buy, costs $250. When you add up the equipment required, you'd be at $1000 if it had no use other than INSTEON remote control.

SmartLinc is especially convenient if you already have a Smartphone with a good web browser and a WiFi network in your home—in that case, it's your least expensive option. Otherwise, consider the RemoteLinc.

DECISION POINT: SMARTLINC

⇒ Mark "SL" on your plans near your wireless router if you plan to use a SmartLinc web controller, "EZS" if you plan to use an EZSrve, or "ISY" if you plan to use an ISY-99i.

Using a Universal Remote

You can control INSTEON lighting from any universal infrared remote by installing an IRLinc infrared receiver. The IRLinc option is pretty easy to use if your primary remote needs are based around your television. Like all infrared solutions, IRLincs are specific to a single room and purpose—specifically, dimming the lights when you turn on your television. They're not all that useful for other purposes, but they're terrific for solving the home theater problem.

The SimpleHomeNet EZUIRT is a very similar device that is also capable of working as an "IR Blaster" in order to transmit commands to A/V equipment.

I have my IRLinc configured to bring down the room lights when I press the Play button on my Harmony 890 Universal remote, and to bring them back up to 50% when we turn the A/V system off. It also controls the A/V cooling fans. We don't use the IRLinc much beyond that because it is difficult to find use cases that always apply irrespective of who is using the TV and what time of day it is—and because we don't carry a universal remote around in our pocket.

DECISION POINT: UNIVERSAL INFRARED REMOTE LINKING

⇒ Mark "IRL" on your plans next to where you will place your television if you intend to use an IRLinc for remote control.

RemoteLinc

For most people, the RemoteLinc is the lowest-cost, simplest, and most convenient solution to the remote control problem. It's wireless so it works through walls and has a range large enough to cover most homes. Like most remotes, it always seems to be somewhere else when you need it, and it is limited to six switches, which means your choice of any six devices, scenes, or paths.

> I use the RemoteLinc to control the outdoor lighting on our deck when we're outside. I can bring it back in the house, and we avoided installing outdoor switches.

If you have Access Points in your INSTEON system for phase bridging or for receiving wireless motion sensor signals, you should strongly consider adding a RemoteLinc to your system. They're simple to use and very handy.

DECISION POINT: REMOTELINC

⇒ Mark "RL" in your living room area. Also mark "AP" somewhere nearby the living room an in any other distant area you intend to control with RemoteLincs.

Kitchen

The primary use for INSTEON in the kitchen is lighting control. Kitchens typically have a number of utility lights, so consider putting KeypadLinc controllers nearby your counters so you can easily control any of them from wherever you work.

Think about your use cases before you purchase automation devices. For example, while you could use a TimerLinc to control a coffee maker to automatically turn on and begin brewing coffee at sunrise, it would be far less expensive to simply get a coffee maker that has a timer. Use INSTEON when you can't get appliances that have superior automation functionality built in, or when you need the automation to work together with other devices.

One nice thing you can do with INSTEON is easily retrofit lighting where you want it. For example, you probably have counter-level outlets in your kitchen, but you may not have under-counter lighting. Running a circuit through walls to a switch would be expensive and would mean repairing a considerable amount of drywall.

But you can easily install under-counter lighting and connect them to near-by outlets that would typically be so close you could simply fish the wiring behind the drywall from the counter lights to the outlet. To control the lights, install an InLineLinc relay in the wall behind the outlet and link it to any KeypadLinc.

You can also use this technique to gain more control over a string of lights that are all currently controlled via a single switch. For example, in our kitchen we have a set of six fluorescent recessed lights (cans) on a single switch, which lights up the kitchen quite a bit more than we usually want later in the evening. So I removed a can cover and discovered that I could easily place an InLineLinc relay in the ceiling in series with the last three cans to control them separately. Now we can turn on three of the cans or an additional three with separate buttons on a KeypadLinc.

DECISION POINT: ADDING LIGHTING CONTROL WITH InLineLincs

⇒ Mark your plans with "ILR" or "ILR" at each fixture on a loop that you would prefer to directly control with a switch button. You can also replace existing gangs of switches with InLineLincs and a single KeypadLinc if you have switches in poorly planned areas. Consider plating over exterior switches and installing InLineLincs in those locations as well, with a RemoteLinc to control lighting when you are outside.

Offices

Offices typically have a considerable number of devices that either don't sleep or continue to draw a considerable amount of power while in sleep mode. You can use an ApplianceLinc to cut power to these devices when not in use can lower your energy use if their sleep mode power draw exceeds six watts in sum. Linking the main light switch to the ApplianceLinc to light up your office when you enter.

You can't just arbitrarily cut power to your computer using an ApplianceLinc, nor should you cut power to many directly attached peripherals or the devices involved in creating your computer network. Some devices, such as printers and monitors, are safe to automatically shut off when you're not using them.

SAVING POWER IN THE OFFICE

OFFICE EQUIPMENT THAT SHOULD NOT BE POWER INTERRUPTED

⇒ Home Computers or Uninterruptible Power Supplies (UPS).
⇒ USB Connected peripheral devices such as External Hard disks
⇒ DSL/Cable Routers, Wireless Access Points, and your DSL/Cable modem
⇒ Ethernet hubs and switches

DEVICES YOU CAN SAFELY CUT POWER TO WHEN UNUSED

⇒ Printers and multifunction devices, even when USB attached
⇒ Monitors
⇒ Scanners
⇒ Fax machines

Split the devices between different power strips—one for devices that remain on, and one for devices that can be switched off. Put the ApplianceLinc on the power strip powering devices that can be turned off.

DECISION POINT: SAVING POWER WITH APPLIANCELINC

⇒ Mark "AL" on your plans in your office area.

Bedrooms

INSTEON is especially convenient in the bedroom. Being able to light up areas outside the bedroom at night is a nice convenience. Path lighting is also especially important in bedrooms both as the end-point to turn paths off and to light paths if you have to get up in the middle of the night. Being able to bring up all your external lights from bedside if you hear something outside provides peace of mind.

One non-obvious issue with installing INSTEON devices in Bedrooms is the amount of light generated by LEDs and keypad backlights. When I setup our Master Bedroom, I didn't give any thought to the LED issue. In most of the house, the LEDs from INSTEON Devices make for nice ambient night lighting, but the first night that my wife and I tried to sleep in the Master bedroom the lights kept waking both of us. Our room was lit up like a Christmas scene with light from four SwitchLinc Dimmers, two KeypadLincs, an ApplianceLinc, and an Elk security keypad.

The next day was spent covering LEDs with electrical tape and configuring brightness levels in the security keypad device firmware. I ordered black opaque key change kits for the KeypadLincs to dim them (which worked perfectly). You may also want to consider ICON INSTEON switches which have only a single amber LED for bedrooms.

Master Bedroom

Master bedrooms typically don't have light switches installed near the bed. Using a plug-in INSTEON controller such as the ControlLinc, a KeypadLinc in a tabletop enclosure, or a IES TouchScreen in a tabletop enclosure provides a very simple plug-in controller that can be used to turn off all the lights in the house, control lights in children's rooms, turn off all the lights in the room, control television lights or any appliances that leave annoying "off" lights on at night.

DECISION POINT: BEDSIDE LIGHTING CONTROL

⇒ Mark "KLE" on your plans for a KeypadLinc with Enclosure, or "CL" for ControlLinc, near an outlet by a bedside table.

> I use an ApplianceLinc on my clock radio to "unplug" it at night so its bright display doesn't keep me up. Its internal battery keeps the time, and a time-of-day event programmed in HouseLinc turns it back on in time for its alarm to go off in the morning.

Bedrooms

We use INSTEON to control the lights in our children's bedrooms primary to turn them back off when they turn them on. We also bring them up to 50% in our "carry the kids to bed" path that we can turn on from the Garage.

We also control the ceiling and appliance fans and the lamps in my daughter's rooms using LampLinc and ApplianceLinc modules. This allows me to turn off fans remotely once they've gone to sleep.

While it may be possible to control fan speed using a SwitchLinc Dimmer, the "power chopping" method used in SwitchLincs will cause fan motors to hum, can cause the dimmer to hum, and will shorten the life of both. Electronic dimmers are for use only with incandescent lights and are not designed to control inductive loads such as fans.

DECISION POINT: BEDROOM ACCESSORIES
⇒ Mark "AL" near an outlet on your prints for every appliance fan you intend to run in a bedroom.
⇒ Mark "LL" near an outlet on your plans for every lamp you intend to run in a bedroom.

Guest Quarters

It's actually probably not wise to go crazy with INSTEON devices in guest quarters, because most people don't know what to expect from a smart-home system. Your use cases and programming is easy for you to remember, but actually a bit hard to teach, especially for people who won't be in your house for very long. Also, you probably don't want guest lights to go off when you issue "all off" group commands.

Because guests have a large degree of autonomy in their actions, it is probably best to leave guest rooms out of your INSTEON design.

> We have an accessory unit in our home, with no INSTEON devices installed. This prevents "strange" behavior from misunderstood or mis-programmed switches or lights from affecting our guests.

Passageways & Halls

Although passageways and halls might not seem particularly important for lighting, they are places where lights typically are left on because they're often not wired conveniently. Putting INSTEON switches on hall lights also allows them to be incorporated correctly into path lighting.

Entries and Exits

Entries are the perfect place to put KeypadLincs in place of typical switches. By providing a number of control buttons, you can enable path lighting, turn on interior scenes, and shut off all the exterior lights from a single location.

Garage

Garages are often the most common entryway to the house. As with other entryways, you will probably want to put a KeypadLinc at the doorway between the Garage and the house. You should also consider putting the garage lights on a timer.

You can use driveway sensors or motion sensors to pick up the presence of an incoming car. You'll have to think about how to tell the difference between an arriving car and a departing car, however.

> Chapter 4 highlights a number of ways to detect the garage door opening.

DECISION POINT: LIGHTING FROM THE CAR

⇒ Mark "IO" on your prints at an outlet inside your garage.

Bathrooms

Bathrooms are simple: Put the fan on a SwitchLinc Timer, and put the light(s) on a typical SwitchLinc. Then Link the fan to the Light. This way, when you turn the light and fan on using the fan switch, they will both turn off after 15 minutes or some other programmable time. When you turn only the light on, the timer is not enabled and the light will stay on indefinitely. Remember to tell everyone how that simple system works.

DECISION POINT: BATHROOM TIMERS

⇒ Mark "SLT" next to the fan light switch for a SwitchLinc timer (or KLT for an eight button timer)

⇒ Mark "SLR" (relay) or "SLD" (dimmer) as appropriate for the bathroom light(s).

Utility Rooms

Utility rooms that are not normally occupied should all be place on either timers or motion sensors to ensure that lights are turned off throughout the house.

Utility rooms include:
- Closets
- Attics
- Utility rooms
- Storage Rooms
- Laundry

> Save money by putting lights in rooms that are not normally occupied on typical timer or motion sensors rather than INSTEON switches. There is very little gain to using INSTEON in rooms where lights are normally off.

As an alternative, you can create an event timer in a home automation controller, HouseLinc, a web controller, or an INSTEON PLC to turn off all utility room lights at midnight. This ensures that even if they are left on, they're all turned off at night and you won't leave a light on pointlessly for more than a day.

DECISION POINT: UTILITY ROOM TIMERS

⇒   Mark "SLT" next to the light switch in each utility room.

Exterior Lighting and Outdoors

INSTEON really shines when it comes to outdoor lighting. INSTEON provides the ability to control lights in outbuildings from a distance, to replace outside switches with RemoteLincs, and to provide time-of-day control for landscaping.

Entry, Exterior, and Landscape Lighting

Exterior lights should be placed on typical SwitchLincs inside the home near an entry. This will provide the ability to turn off all the exterior lights at once and provide time-of-day events to turn them on at dusk and off at midnight or dawn.

Circuits with multiple 300w flood lamps should be controlled by SwitchLinc Relays or by 1000w SwitchLinc dimmers. Typical SwitchLinc dimmers are rated for 600w and would be maxed out from two flood lamps.

DECISION POINT: FLOODLIGHTS

⇒   Mark "SLDK" next to the switch for high wattage outdoor lights.

Decks and Patios

Decks and patios can be placed on typical SwitchLincs or even plated-over InLineLinc relays inside the home near the back door. Then use an Access

Point and a RemoteLinc, or a web-based controller and your WiFi controller to manage the deck lights when you're out.

DECISION POINT: DECK & PATIO LIGHTS

⇒ Mark "SLR" next to each of your deck and patio lights. If they're exterior and you are doing a major remodel or new construction, have the electricians move them to the interior of the home.

⇒ Mark "AP and RL" next to an outlet close to the deck on the interior of the home.

Outbuildings

Put all the lights in your outbuildings on SwitchLinc timers. That way they can be controlled using paths from inside your home as you're going out to them, and will automatically shut off when you aren't using them. Eight button SwitchLinc timers make a great choice when you stay in a building for differing lengths of time.

Also consider putting major appliances that might be left on in outbuildings (such as compressors, fans, etc.) on ApplianceLincs so you can shut them down remotely.

DECISION POINT: OUTBUILDING CONTROL

⇒ Mark "KLT" next to each light switch in your outbuildings.

⇒ Mark "AL" next to outlets that will be plugged into appliances that may be left on unintentionally.

Pools

Pool lighting should be controlled using INSTEON 1000w dimmers. Pool lighting is typically higher wattage than regular lights.

Pool heaters and pumps can be controlled using the SimpleHomeNet EZSwitch 30 220v relays, allowing you to turn the heaters and pumps on and off using INSTEON events.

⇒ Mark "SLDK" next to the pool lighting switch.

⇒ Mark "EZ3" next to the pool pump switch.

Irrigation

SimpleHomeNet makes a line of irrigation valve controllers that can be programmed with timers to perform all of your irrigation watering like a typical irrigation timer and can also be programmed to respond to seasonal, time-of-day, or other INSTEON events. Their current model as of this writing is the EZFlora.

They lack on-device user interfaces however, and are not weather proof. Because they must be programmed using computer software, it probably makes more sense to go with a standard irrigation timer until you have an INSTEON system that is fully established.

DECISION POINT: INSTEON IRRIGATION CONTROL

⇒ Mark your plans with "EZF" at an exterior outlet with a waterproof enclosure near your exterior irrigation valves.

Determining which devices will be required

Now that you've gone through your home plans room-by-room and switch-by-switch, you have your installation plan and the full count of exactly which devices you'll need.

Using a copy of the next page (or better yet, create a spreadsheet based on it), go through your plans and count the number of each INSTEON device code you've marked on your plans.

Next, look up the current cost of each INSTEON device at www.smarthome.com and fill in the price column. Multiply the quantity of devices total by the price column to come up with an item total, and then sum the item total column to come up with your entire installation budget.

Code	Device	Cost	Qty	Total
KLR	KeypadLinc Relay	$70		
KLD	KeypadLinc Dimmer	$70		
KLDE	KeypadLinc Dimmer with Enclosure	$80		
SLR	SwitchLinc Relay	$46		
SLD	SwitchLinc Dimmer	$46		
SLDK	SwitchLinc Dimmer, 1000w	$70		
AL	ApplianceLinc	$35		
LL	LampLinc	$35		
HPB	Hardwired phase bridge	$25		
PPB	Plug-in phase bridge	$40		
PLM	Powerline Modem, Serial	$60		
PLC	Powerline Controller, USB	$70		
WEB	SmartLinc	$120		
IO	I/OLinc (cost per each I/O)	$46		
MS	Motion Sensor	$35		
SNS	EZSnsRF	$135		
AP	Access Point (need 2 to bridge)	$40		
TS	Thermostat	$160		
WC	Window Controller	$350		
IRL	IRLinc	$100		
RL	RemoteLinc	$60		
ILR	InLineLinc Relay	$46		
ILD	InLineLinc Dimmer	$46		
CL	ControlLinc	$35		
EZX	EZX-10RF	$125		
EZS	EZSrve	$210		
SLT	SwitchLinc Timer	$60		
KLT	KeypadLinc Timer	$65		
EZ3	EZSwitch 30	$115		
EZF	EZFlora	$125		
ISY	ISY-99i	$400		
Budget Total				

Table 5.x: Calculating an INSTEON system budget

I've not included the cost of sophisticated home automation controllers or any home automation software beyond HouseLinc and the very low cost embedded web controllers in this planning chapter because those devices change very rapidly and because I strongly believe that you should establish your INSTEON system and get your basic links programmed prior to deciding that you need a home automation controller.

> The prices in the preceding table were valid at the time of this writing, but are for budgetary purposes only and will change without notice or modification of this book.

Budgeting and Ordering

Taking your device counts and budgets and converting them to an order online is easy. Most of the devices are sold at smarthome.com. The remainder of this chapter gives advice on ordering strategies and tips to reduce your overall cost.

Order and install in small batches and a number of increments

By making your first order rather small and specific in purpose, you can be absolutely certain that everything works they way you want before you make an entire order. You're also far less likely to accidentally over-order this way, and you can take advantage of deals that appear periodically on the smarthome.com website.

When you order from Smarthome.com, they frequently send out follow up e-mails with a coupon code to save 10% or so off your next order. By ordering incrementally, you can take advantage of these deals. You'll also want to configure your orders in increments of $200—that's the price point at which Smarthome.com frequently offers free ground shipping.

Hold off on high-cost devices until you know you need them

Install the basics—lighting and appliance control—and get them configured before you invest in expensive devices like LCD keypads, web controllers, or a home automation controller. You'll likely find that you won't need the more expensive controllers after all, or that low cost devices such as an EZSrve or SmartLinc will do what you need.

With any large installation, you will want to use SmartLabs' HouseLinc software to manage links between devices more easily than manual linking. While HouseLinc is great for programming, it's also possible to use it for direct light control, although the user interface is not built for that purpose.

Look for lower cost versions

SmartLabs occasionally makes lower cost versions of their devices. For example, they've periodically released batches of KeypadLinc keypads that use lower cost amber LEDs rather than White and are 25% less expensive. If you want amber anyway or you're going to put opaque keys over the device, you can save money by looking for these kinds of deals.

Minimize the number of devices in your plan

You don't necessarily have to use INSTEON to control every light in your house. Outside lights, bathroom lights that are already on motion-sensors or timers, closet and utility room lights, and bathroom fans are all examples of devices that you would probably not include in a path or scene for lighting.

Think of it this way: If you wouldn't want to turn the light "on" when you aren't actually in the room, you probably don't need INSTEON control over that light or device. A simple and less expense timer or motion sensor switch will do to ensure that the light isn't left on.

ICON

ICON switches and appliance controls are lower priced INSTEON devices. They typically cost 25% to 33% less than their "Linc" counterparts, and they achieve this cost savings by using less expensive components: Magnetic relays rather than silicon controlled relays, lower cost amber LEDs rather than white, and no pass-through power outlet. They're a great way to reduce the cost of an INSTEON project without sacrificing functionality.

> You won't want to mix ICON installed switches and INSTEON switches in the same room. The style and light colors do not match, and it gives the room a "random electronics" look rather than a coherent design.

Summary

While INSTEON is simplest for specific purposes, it's easier than competing technologies to plan for the entire home as well. Whole home planning and budgeting for INSTEON requires a copy of mockup of your electrical blue-prints, and some thought about the automation problems you want to solve.

You should perform your installation in an initial phase consisting of installed switch devices, and then individual purchases of the additional devices you want to add for particular purposes and more complex automation.

Save money by limiting the rooms in your house where you use automation, growing your installation over time, and selecting lower cost devices.

Chapter 6
Installation & Troubleshooting

INSTEON is a highly reliable system designed with numerous resiliency and fault tolerance measures built in. Amongst its primary fault tolerance features is its distributed nature—there are no single points of failure, so there's literally no possibility that an entire INSTEON deployment will fail. At worst, only parts of an INSTEON system will fail to function.

But as with any complex system, failures occur.

This chapter provides generic troubleshooting advice for all INSTEON devices and installations. You should also follow the specific troubleshooting steps provided in the user's guide for the INSTEON device you are having trouble with.

I've presented the troubleshooting measures in this chapter in the order that you should perform them for an arbitrary problem—not in order of how common the failures are. The most common failure in a new INSTEON installation is failure to couple phases properly. But once phase coupling is done, it's done; there are rarely future problems with phase coupling, especially in systems that use hardwired phase couplers.

TERMINOLOGY: INSTALLING INSTEON DEVICES

2-Wire Switch—A junction box that contains only LINE and LOAD wires with no NEUTRAL wire.

Fixture-Switch—A circuit wired such that the power travels from the circuit panel to the fixture, and from the fixture to the switch.

Inductive Load—A magnetic load such as a low-voltage transformer or a ceiling fan.

Null Switch—An INSTEON switch that controls no load, because the switch location was originally a traveler from a three-way switch or a switched outlet.

Switch-Fixture—A circuit wired such that the power travels from the circuit panel to the switchbox, and from junction box to the fixture.

Switched Outlet—a power outlet that runs through a switch because it was originally designed to switch a lamp.

Wiring for INSTEON

Many INSTEON devices require no installation at all—they are plug and play. You can do a lot with INSTEON without touching your electrical wiring at all, but if you want to control installed fixtures, you will have to install wired in INSTEON devices.

Insteon SwitchLinc and InLineLinc switches have three wires: HOT, NEUTRAL, and LOAD. In all cases you simply wire the corresponding NEUTRAL, HOT, and LOAD wires in the junction box to the switch. It can sometimes be difficult to determine which wire is hot and which is load, but a voltage tester can tell you with certainty.

INSTEON OutletLinc devices are wired simply to NEUTRAL and HOT, because they're switched load is the outlet itself. They are a simple replacement for traditional outlets.

INSTEON operates over typical house wiring. Even in the case that you have two-wire switch-legs with no neutrals, SmartLabs has switches that will work for you.

The biggest change most people will have to make to their wiring is re-wiring three-way switches. Because there are many different ways that a three-way switch might be wired, correctly wiring them for INSTEON can be confusing. This section demystifies the three-way wiring problem and provides detailed instructions for identifying and correctly wiring three-way switches for INSTEON.

Identifying neutrals

Typical switches are not wired to neutral, but INSTEON switches have to be. When you open the switch junction box, remove the screws from the switch and pull it out. Behind the switch, you'll see multiple white (typically) wires twisted together with a wirenut on them. These are the neutrals in your switchbox. To install an INSTEON switch, remove the wirenut from the bundle, add the white wire from the INSTEON switch to the bundle, and screw the wirenut back down onto the bundle.

If the bundle of neutrals becomes too large for a single wirenut, get another wirenut, split the bundle of wires into two equal groups, and cut a 3" length of white 14-gauge solid core wire to connect the two bundles electrically (You can cut this from one of the neutrals in the switch box if it is long enough). Screw down wirenuts on both bundles such that the 3" wire is screwed into each of the two to ensure that they remain correctly connected.

Identifying Line vs. Load

Identifying neutral and ground is easy. Unfortunately, the line=black and load=red convention is actually not often adhered to. In my home, which is brand new, the colors properly identify line and load about half the time—completely randomly, in other words. Furthermore, in manual on/off switches and many dimmers, line and load can be safely reversed, so their position on the switch you are replacing does not necessarily indicate which is which.

Do not presume that you can match red-to-red and black-to-black with your INSTEON device. If you are not certain which line is line and which is load, use a voltage sensor to determine it. The surest way to determine line is to energize the circuit and use a voltage sensor to find the hot line. Unfortunately this can be dangerous, so be very careful with exposed wires.

In my testing, INSTEON relay based devices work irrespective of whether LINE and LOAD are swapped, although they tend to switch with a slight delay if they are swapped.

TESTING FOR LINE VOLTAGE

⇒ Wear leather palmed electrical gloves
⇒ Make sure all white neutrals are bundled together with a single wirenut (or two directly connected wire-nuts)
⇒ Make sure all ground lines are wired to ground
⇒ Cap all the red and black load and line candidate wires individually with small wirenuts before you re-energize the circuit so that no bare wires are exposed anywhere
⇒ Connect the common lead of your voltage meter to ground using the alligator clip lead
⇒ If you are using a multimeter, set it to AC voltage and to the 100 volt range
⇒ Check voltage one wire at a time by inserting the positive (red) needle probe of your voltmeter into the wirenut. If necessary, remove the wirenut, check the voltage by touching the bare wire, and replace the wirenut. All the lines will read some small voltage, but only hot lines will read over 100 volts.
⇒ Label hot using black electrical tape
⇒ Label lines you've identified as load with red electrical tape

Dealing with 2-wire switches

If you don't have neutral wires in the junction box, you'll need to order special two-wire INSTEON switches. Two wire switches split the switch plate and the relay or dimmer so you can place the relay at the fixture in the ceiling, and re-wire the traveler going to the switch to include both hot and neutral, rather than hot and load.

INSTALLING AN INSTEON 2-WIRE SWITCH

⇒ De-energize the circuit at the circuit breaker.

⇒ Wear leather gloves.

⇒ At the junction box, remove the old switch and wire the 2-wire switch plate to HOT and the former LOAD wire which will now be designated NEUTRAL.

⇒ At the fixture, wire both HOT wires and the LINE wire from the 2-wire switch together with a wirenut. Wire the NEUTRAL, the former LOAD wire now designated NEUTRAL, and the NEUTRAL wire from the 2-wire switch together using a wirenut. Wire the LOAD wire from the 2-wire switch to the fixture load.

Two-wire switches are more difficult to install because you have to rewire both at the switch and at the junction box.

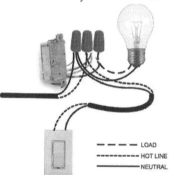

Figure 6.1: 2-Wire INSTEON switch wiring

Rewiring switched outlets

When you move to INSTEON, you may no longer want to have outlets wired to switches because you can use INSTEON to control lamps and other appliances anywhere in your house. In this case, simply remove the switch and use wirenuts to connect hot to load in the switch junction box.

152

If you want to retain the switch for some other purpose, just put an INSTEON switch in place of the original switch by wiring the line wire into the hot-line wirenut and wiring the neutral. Place a wirenut over the load wire, which will remain unused. Now you have an INSTEON switch that does not directly control a load but which can be programmed to control any INSTEON device in your home.

If your house lacks neutrals in the junction box, you could rewire the outlet to bring neutral back to the switch junction box on the load lead and use that to wire an INSTEON switch.

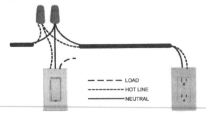

Figure 6.2: Re-wiring a switched outlet for INSTEON

REWIRING A SWITCHED OUTLET

⇒ Using a multimeter, identify the LINE (120v), NEUTRAL (0V), and LOAD (0V When off, 120V when on) lines.

⇒ De-energize the circuit at the circuit breaker. Turn the light switch on and ensure that it remains off to be certain that the correct circuit has been de-energized.

⇒ Wear leather gloves.

⇒ In the switch junction box, remove the original switch.

⇒ Wire the GROUND wire to the bare copper GROUND wire on the INSTEON device using a wirenut. Repeat this process for the LOAD, NEUTRAL, and LINE wires in that order. NEUTRAL will probably be wired into a bundle with other NEUTRAL wires. Ensure that no bare wires are exposed below any wirenuts except the GROUND wires.

⇒ Re-energize the circuit at the circuit breaker.

⇒ Test the INSTEON switch to ensure that it correctly drives the primary load.

⇒ Push the wirenut circuits back into the junction box and install the INSTEON switch into the junction box.

If you are building a home new construction, don't install switched outlets. You'll use INSTEON devices to accomplish the same thing in a much more controllable fashion.

Re-wiring energized circuits

It is my strong advice that you never wire an INSTEON device without de-energizing the circuit. If, for whatever reason, you've determined to do so anyway, the following steps are the safest way to do so.

REWIRING A SWITCHED OUTLET

⇒ De-energize the circuit at the circuit breaker if at all possible.

⇒ Wear leather gloves. Never, under any circumstances, should you work on a live circuit without wearing insulating leather gloves made specifically for electrical use.

⇒ Prepare the INSTEON device by pulling out the set switch by 1/8" and ensuring that it stays extended. This will keep the device powered off and prevent sparking while you install it.

⇒ Unscrew the LINE or HOT wire from the switch, being exceptionally careful not to allow the exposed wire touch anything. Cap the wire off with a wirenut that will identify it as LINE. Repeat this procedure for NEUTRAL, LOAD, and GROUND in that order.

⇒ Remove the wirenut from GROUND and wire it to the INSTEON device, being careful not to touch the wire to any thing other than the intended wire and wirenut. Repeat this process for LOAD, NEUTRAL, and LINE in that order. Be absolutely certain that no bare wire is exposed outside of a wirenut for any wire except GROUND.

⇒ Push in the INSTEON set switch to power on the INSTEON device. Test its proper installation, and install the switch into the junction box.

Re-wiring three-way switches

If you have an existing three-way switch with switch-legs, you will have to re-wire the switches to ensure that the junction boxes all receive power at all times. If you don't re-wire the switches, you could wind up with INSTEON devices that loses power and cannot respond to signals.

This section is going to seem completely confusing if you are just casually reading. Read through this section carefully when you actually have the problem of re-wiring a three-way switch—you can skip it for now unless you are very interested in the nuances of three-way switch wiring.

Once your switch is rewired, you'll have one switch that controls the load and one "null switch" that controls nothing—its load line will be capped off and disconnected. You can either plate over the old switch, or install an INSTEON switch that is cross-linked to the load control switch in order to mimic the previous three way circuit.

If the location of the null switch is near a high-traffic doorway, they're the perfect place to put eight-button KeypadLincs in my opinion. INSTEON switches always control their local load, so the "A" button on a KeypadLinc is normally dedicated to the local load. In locations where you are not controlling a load, the "A" button can be freely assigned to any purpose you want.

Determining how a three-way switch is wired

Typical three-way switches have two switch poles and a "COMMON" terminal that will be differently colored (usually green). When the switch is thrown, common connects to one of the two switch poles.

No matter how a three-way circuit is wired, COMMON on one switch will be wired to HOT. This is called the power-feed switch. COMMON on the other switch will be wired to fixture LOAD. This is called the fixture feed switch.

> Circuits are identified by the order in which power from the circuit breaker panel is wired to components.

The possible ways that a 3-way switch could be wired are:
- FSS-T (Fixture-switch-switch with traveler)
- FSS (Fixture-switch-switch without traveler)
- SSF-T (Switch-switch-fixture with traveler)
- SFS-T (Switch-fixture-switch with traveler)
- SFS (Switch-fixture-switch without traveler)

It is actually pretty easy to determine how a three-way circuit is wired once you've determined which switch is the power feed switch and how many cables are wired to each switch and fixture.

Using the following table and procedure, you should be able to determine exactly how any 3-way switch is wired. Once you've determined how the switch is wired, you can use the instructions in the remainder of this section to re-wire the switch for INSTEON.

DETERMINE HOW A THREE-WAY SWITCH IS WIRED

PREPARING TO DETERMINE THE CIRCUIT TYPE

⇒ Open the fixture, and determine whether the fixture is wired to one two-conductor cable (label the fixture "1 cable"), or to two different cables (label the fixture "2 cable").

⇒ Leaving the circuit breaker energized, place both switches in the OFF position such that the fixture light is off.

⇒ Remove the faceplates from both of the three-way switches.

⇒ Using an alligator clip black negative probe, clip the black voltmeter lead to ground.

⇒ On a three-way switch, the oddly colored screw terminal is the common terminal. Identify the common terminal on each switch.

⇒ Using a needle probe tip on the red positive probe of the voltmeter, touch the common terminal.

⇒ If the common terminal is hot, this is the power feed switch. Label this switch as "Power Feed." If both switches seem to be the power feed switch, then one of the switches is on. Switch the switches until you can find a state where the light is off and only one of the switches has power to the common terminal of the 3-way switch. This is the power feed switch.

⇒ Inspect both switches to determine whether all conductors wired to the switch come from a single cable, or if the conductors wired to the switch come from two different cables. Label switches wired to a single cable as "1 Cable" and switches wired to two cables as "2 cable."

SSF-T: Switch-Switch-Fixture with Traveler

⇒ If both switches are labeled "2 cable," then this circuit is wired SSFT. The fixture feed switch is the switch opposite of the power feed switch. The fixture will be labeled "1 cable." Skip the rest of this procedure as you have identified the circuit.

FSS: Fixture-Switch-Switch

⇒ If both switches are labeled "1 cable," then this circuit is wired FSS. The power feed switch is the same switch as the fixture feed switch. The fixture will be labeled "2 Cable." Skip the rest of this procedure as you have identified the circuit.

SFS: Switch-Fixture-Switch

⇒ If the power feed switch is labeled "2 cable," then this circuit is wired SFS. The power feed switch is the same as the fixture feed switch. The fixture will be labeled "2 Cable." Skip the rest of this procedure as you have identified the circuit.

SFS-T: Switch-Fixture-Switch with Traveler

⇒ If the fixture is labeled "1 cable," then the circuit is wired switch-fixture-switch with a traveler. Skip the rest of this procedure as you have identified the circuit.

FSS-T: Fixture-Switch-Switch with Traveler

⇒ If the fixture is labeled "2 cable," then the circuit is wired fixture-switch-switch with a traveler. Skip the rest of this procedure as you have identified the circuit.

In the table below, power-feed switch refers to the switch with HOT wired to common, fixture-feed switch refers to the switch with COMMON wired to fixture LOAD. "1 cable" refers to a device being wired to conductors from a single cable, and "2 cable" refers to a device being wired to conductors in separate cables.

Now that you've determined how your three-way switch is wired, you can convert the wiring for INSTEON.

INSTEON requires that all junction boxes be powered at all times, so in circuits with travelers, you will convert a traveler wire to be a power feed wire to carry power to the second junction box in order to power the INSTEON switch.

	Fixture	Power-feed switch	Fixture-feed switch
SSF-T	1 cable	2 cable	2 cable
FSS	2 cable	1 cable	1 cable
SFS	2 cable	2 cable	1 cable
SFS-T	1 cable	1 cable	2 cable
FSS-T	2 cable	1 cable	2 cable

Table 6.x: 3-way switch characteristics

Once you've converted the traveler to carry power, the switch you identified as the fixture feed switch will be wired to control the load directly, and the other switch will have its load wire capped off and will not directly control any load—you'll use INSTEON links to re-create the three-way functionality.

Using the wiring type you've determined from the above procedure, select the correct procedure from the four options below to rewire your circuit.

Re-wiring SFS for INSTEON

In a switch-fixture-switch circuit with no traveler, the two switches are wired together in the fixture, thus eliminating the need for a traveler wire going from one switch to another. Rather than a traveler the fixture feed switch is on a switch-leg.

REWIRING SFS CIRCUITS FOR INSTEON

⇒ De-energize the circuit at the circuit breaker and remove the existing switches from both junction boxes.

⇒ At the power-feed junction box, wire both white NEUTRAL wires and the SwitchLinc NEUTRAL together. Wire all three black HOT wires together. Wire the LOAD wire going to the fixture to the LOAD wire on the SwitchLinc. Be sure to correctly identify HOT and LOAD using either the correct wire colors (black=hot, red=load) or with electrical tape.

⇒ At the light fixture, there will be two three-conductor cables. Wire both cable neutrals and the fixture NEUTRAL together. Wire the fixture to the LOAD line from the power feed switch. Wire the two HOT wires in the cables together. Cap off the third unused wire in the cable going to the fixture feed switch with a wirenut.

⇒ At the fixture feed junction box, wire the HOT and NEUTRAL wires to the SwitchLinc, and cap off the unused wire in the cable with a wire nut. Cap off the unused LOAD wire on the INSTEON switch with a wirenut.

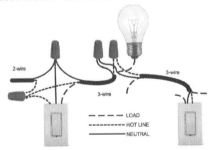

Figure 6.3: Re-wiring SFS switches for INSTEON

In an SFS circuit with no traveler, you'll re-wire the power-feed switch box to control the light, connecting HOT, NEUTRAL, and LOAD to the appropriate wires going to the fixture. In the fixture, you'll wire the light to HOT and LOAD, and also wire HOT and NEUTRAL to the cable going down to the second switch.

In the second switch junction box, you'll wire the switch to HOT and NEUTRAL, capping off the LOAD wire and program a cross-link with the first switch to control the light.

Re-wiring SFS-T circuits for INSTEON

In a Switch-Fixture-Switch circuit with traveler circuit, power actually comes into the same junction box as the fixture feed but hot is wired over to the second switch making the switch at the end of the traveler the power feed switch.

This circuit is easy to re-wire: Simply replace the fixture feed switch with an INSTEON switch, and then wire the traveler for HOT and NEUTRAL. In the second junction box, wire the INSTEON switch to HOT and NEUTRAL leaving the LOAD wire capped off. Use a programmed crosslink between the two switches to control the three-way light.

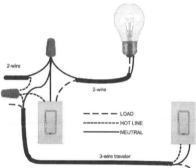

Figure 6.4: Re-wiring SFS-T switches for INSTEON

REWIRING SFS-T CIRCUITS FOR INSTEON

⇒ De-energize the circuit at the circuit breaker and remove the existing switches from both junction boxes.

⇒ At the fixture-feed junction box, wire both white NEUTRAL wires and the SwitchLinc NEUTRAL together. Wire HOT to the black HOT wire in the traveler cable and to the SwitchLinc HOT. Wire the LOAD wire going to the fixture to the LOAD wire on the SwitchLinc. Be sure to correctly identify HOT and LOAD using either the correct wire colors (black=hot, red=load) or with electrical tape.

⇒ At the Power-feed junction box, wire the INSTEON device to NEUTRAL and HOT, using a wirenut to cap off the unused LOAD wire.

Re-wiring SSF-T circuits for INSTEON

In a switch-switch-fixture with traveler circuit, power feeds to one of the switches, through a traveler to the other switch, and then to the fixture. This is the most common type of three-way switch circuit.

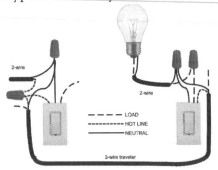

Figure 6.5: Re-wiring a SSF-T switch for INSTEON

To convert this switch to INSTEON, the traveler is converted to carry power from the power feed switch to the fixture feed switch, the power feed switch load wire is capped off, and the fixture is directly controlled from the fixture feed switch.

REWIRING SSF-T CIRCUITS FOR INSTEON

⇒ De-energize the circuit at the circuit breaker and remove the existing switches from both junction boxes.

⇒ At the power-feed junction box, wire both white NEUTRAL wires and the SwitchLinc NEUTRAL together. Wire all three black HOT wires together. Cap off the unused LOAD wire on the SwitchLinc. Cap off the unused third (red) wire in the traveler cable.

⇒ At the fixture-feed switch, wire the LOAD wire going to the fixture to the LOAD wire on the SwitchLinc.

Re-wiring FSS circuits for INSTEON

In fixture-switch-switch circuits with no traveler, power is fed to the fixture, and a switch-leg goes down to each of two switches.

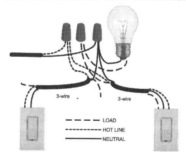

Figure 6.6: Re-wiring an FSS switch for INSTEON

The FSS circuit is easy to convert to INSTEON: Simply wire HOT and NEUTRAL to both switch-legs, and then wire LOAD on the power-feed switch to LOAD on the fixture, capping off LOAD on the other switch.

REWIRING FSS CIRCUITS FOR INSTEON

⇒ At the fixture, wire all three HOT wires together from the three cables in the fixture. Wire all three NEUTRAL wires together along with the NEUTRAL wire for the fixture. Wire the LOAD wire for the fixture to the LOAD wire of either cable, capping off the LOAD wire of the other cable.

⇒ At the fixture wired to LOAD at the fixture, install a SwitchLinc switch according to the normal instructions.

⇒ At the fixture not wired to load, install a SwitchLinc switch capping off the unused LOAD wires on the switch and the cable.

Re-wiring FSS-T circuits for INSTEON

In fixture-switch-switch circuits, power feeds to the fixture, and then down to a switch, through a traveler, and to the final switch.

FSS-T switches are a problem: There are typically only two wires that go from the fixture to the first switch. Because these two wires need to be converted from HOT and LOAD to HOT and NEUTRAL, there is no LOAD wire to carry the switched power back to the light.

The solution is to use an INSTEON InLineLinc in the ceiling with the fixture. In this scenario, HOT and NEUTRAL are sent down the switch-leg to the switch, and also wired into the InLineLinc device. The InLineLinc HOT and LOAD are then wired to the fixture. In the junction boxes, INSTEON switches are wired to HOT and NEUTRAL with the LOAD wire capped off. Finally, link programming is used to control the fixture InLineLinc from the switches.

REWIRING FSS-T CIRCUITS FOR INSTEON

⇒ At the fixture, install an InLineLinc Dimmer or Relay by wiring all three HOT wires together, all three NEUTRAL wires together along with the Fixture light NEUTRAL, and by wiring the InLineLinc LOAD to the Fixture LOAD.

⇒ At each switchbox, wire all NEUTRAL and HOT lines together, and cap off the unused wire in the traveler cable and the unused LOAD wires in both switches.

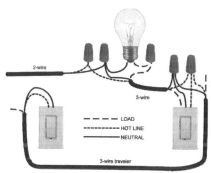

2-wire

3-wire

— — — LOAD
- - - - - HOT LINE
———— NEUTRAL

3-wire traveler

Figure 6.7: Re-wiring FSS-T switches for INSTEON

Hard-wired phase coupling

Hard-wired phase coupling is more reliable than RF phase couplers. SmartLabs emphasizes the RF phase couplers because they're easier to install and can get do-it-yourselfer's up and running with INSTEON very easily. They're an important part of the total INSTEON equation. And since most people "test" INSTEON with a starter kit before they jump in, nearly everyone will own a pair of INSTEON Access Points anyway.

Once you're relying on INSTEON to run your home, install a plug-in phase coupler on any 220V outlet. Or, if you are building a new home or you have room in your breaker panel, have an electrician install a phase coupler in your circuit breaker. Hard-wired phase couplers are very simple and practically failure-proof. They're also more reliable in the long run and not subject to interference, signal fade, or being accidentally unplugged.

Powerline filtering

In my experience, powerline filtering has not been required for the reliable operation of INSTEON devices. But your mileage may vary.

Powerline filtering significantly assists X10 signals. But because all INSTEON devices are repeaters and because INSTEON signals are repeated more than X10 signals, the signal strength becomes higher with each hop, practically ensuring that signals will overwhelm any noise on your lines.

For cases where INSTEON signals have trouble reaching devices when they shouldn't or when it numerous or randomly different delays show that devices are switching later in the INSTEON repetition than they should, and when all devices seem to be equally or randomly affected, and you know that phase coupling is installed and working, you should install a powerline filter at the main point of entry.

Powerline filters attenuate signals on the powerline by coupling a capacitor across the hot legs and neutral. Capacitors "absorb" signals—equipment with large capacitors in power supplies can actually attenuate INSTEON signals in nearby devices, for example—but they are useful when you want to absorb signals. A powerline filter at your main point of entry will reduce noise coming from neighboring homes and prevent your INSTEON signals from traveling out of your house.

Troubleshooting

Once you've installed your INSTEON devices, it's time to test. Testing is simple: Power on the circuit and determine whether the installed INSTEON device's LED turns on. All INSTEON devices have an LED that shows when the device is powered (although ICON switches shut the LED off when the load fixture is turned on, and KeypadLincs have a mode that allows you to shut off the keypad backlighting).

Once you can see that the INSTEON device is powered, turn on the switch and ensure that the load fixture comes on as you expect.

Incomplete Installation

Every INSTEON device has at least one LED that indicates that it is powered. If you have installed an INSTEON device and its LED does not light, it is either wired incorrectly or power has not been applied to the circuit. Follow electrical troubleshooting as described in Chapter 2 to determine the cause, or call an electrician if you cannot determine why a device is not receiving power.

Phase Coupling

Problems with phase coupling appear as typical failure to switch when the controllers and receives are somewhat distant from one another—when they are not on the same phase of your electrical home wiring. Phase coupling problems are usually very consistent: Messages usually don't get through at all when there's a problem with phase coupling, or get through only rarely. Problems with phase coupling are usually immediately obvious.

If you use Access Points to perform phase coupling, there is a chance that these devices may fail. They can also be subject to interference in the 900MHz ISM band, or too far apart for their signals to reliably be received. Failing or intermittent phase coupling issues will appear to be random failure to switch when the controller is distant from the receiver.

Interference in the ISM bands is notoriously difficult to troubleshoot. Many commands will get through, so failures will appear to be completely random. Sometimes you may be able to correlate failure with the source of interference, such as switch failures occurring when you use a 900MHz telephone. But in most cases the source of interference will not be obvious.

Hardwired phase couplers are passive in nature—they contain no complex active electronics and are therefore exceptionally unlikely to ever fail. They also don't use radio frequency to bridge the phases and are therefore entirely immune to interference.

Switch from RF phase coupling to a hardwired phase coupler if message propagation seems to be unreliable.

Signal Propagation

Once you know you have good phase coupling, if you still have any intermittent problems with INSTEON devices randomly in your network, you probably have a signal propagation problem.

The difference in effect from a lack of phase coupling is randomness: Bad phase coupling will typically prevent devices from switching at all, or interfere with a majority of commands—the devices fail to switch with regularity. Powerline condition problems, on the other hand, are much subtler: devices usually switch, but fail to occasionally, and delays or retries are common.

Signal propagation problems happen for three reasons:

- Attenuation—not enough signal power is generated to travel the distance between the transmitter and the receiver
- Filtering—signals are being damped by power conditioning equipment such as uninterruptable power supplies or filtering power strips.
- Noise—signals are being garbled by other transient electrical noise on the powerline.

It's not possible to determine which of these specific problems you might be having without test equipment except by using your intuition and these guidelines:

- If you know you have powerline filters or conditioners in your home, suspect filtering. A common problem is plugging INSTEON devices into power strips that include powerline filters.
- If you have few INSTEON devices (fewer than two per 1000 sq.ft.) and they are distant from one anther, suspect attenuation.
- If you have numerous INSTEON devices (more than two per 1000 sq.ft.) and you know that there are no powerline filtering devices in your path, suspect electrical noise.

Attenuation

The most effective solution to signal attenuation is to add more INSTEON devices to your network. INSTEON devices repeat signals that they hear in lock step. When you have numerous devices repeating the same signal in synchrony, the power of the command signal is greatly increased and it can easily overcome most transient noise and filters.

It's only when you have a very few devices and you are attempting to send signals long distances that you may encounter attenuation problems. Try plugging a few LampLinc or Appliance Link modules around the house between the controller and the receiver to see if the problem goes away. If it does, you need more INSTEON devices to create a reliable network.

Noise

If you've got good phase coupling, only a few devices (less than ten) in your INSTEON system, and you are having random trouble with certain devices receiving commands, you probably have problems with electrical noise. To solve this problem, consider installing a powerline filter at your electrical panel's main point of entry into your house. A powerline filter is essentially a high capacity capacitor that suppresses transient signals from sources outside your home. It also stifles X-10 signals and INSTEON signals that may be travelling from other homes.

Problems stemming from powerline conditions will typically interfere with INSTEON command propagation and express as random command loss—devices that randomly fail to switch. It's not possible to tell command loss due to natural attenuation (signal fade) from command loss due to powerline noise without test equipment, but installing a powerline filter at your electrical main point of entry will squelch noise and certainly won't hurt anything.

Because phase coupling is the most common problem, you should suspect it first. Once you know you have good phase coupling, install a powerline filter to eliminate random failures across a number of devices.

Filters inside the system

While a powerline filter at your electrical main point of entry is a good idea, filters inside your electrical network will interfere with the propagation of INSTEON commands. Power strips generally have powerline filters embedded within them, as do uninterruptable power supplies. It's not always apparent when power strips have filters, but if they have a switch and a fuse, they probably also have a filter.

Use a simple powerline splitter with no active electronic components if you need to connect multiple plug-in INSTEON devices (such as ControlLincs, ApplianceLincs, or LampLincs) into a single wall outlet. If you have other devices you'd like to use a powerstrip with, plug the INSTEON device into power and plug the power strip into its pass-through power port.

Bad Programming

Because INSTEON devices are easy to program, you tend to program them. A lot. And then forget what you've done and why. And then multiple people reprogram the same devices to do different things. And then nobody knows why a switch is behaving the way it behaves.

Bad programming is a fact of life when you do it yourself. Fortunately, it's easy to fix. All of the issues I've personally had with INSTEON devices come down to my own misunderstanding of how to program links initially, and failure to delete links when I've moved devices.

Bad link programming expresses as simple undesired switching: You press the living room light and the kitchen lights also come up. You move an Appliance link and program it to the Kitchen switch, forgetting that it's still linked to a bathroom switch. Now when you turn on the lights in the bathroom, the coffee maker goes on. Of course, this will happen to your spouse who doesn't know anything about the link programming you've done, and suddenly your smarthome system is untrustworthy.

Bad link programming can also express as extra long on times (as half-links are transmitted that will never be responded to) and as flashing LEDs on controllers, which happens when the receiver does not acknowledge a controller signal.

The ease of programming links in INSTEON devices is also an Achilles heel: Because they're easy to install and move around, you do move them around. Because they're easy to program, you program them yourself.

Because you don't have to use a centralized programming tool, you can lose track of what you've done.

There are two solutions to this common problem: Use HouseLinc to keep track of your programming using a computer, or factory reset a device every time you move or repurpose it. The use of HouseLinc is covered in chapter 7.

Factory Resetting

Every INSTEON device has a technique for factory reset. Factory reset erases the link table in the device, ensuring that it will no longer respond to other INSTEON or X-10 controllers until you reprogram it. It is the easiest way to get to a "Known Good" state without using HouseLinc.

Of course, when you lose all your programming, you lose all your programming. You'll have to recreate all the links that involve that device. Also, factory resetting will leave broken links in the remotely linked device as well.

> Factory resetting an INSTEON device removes links from all of its controllers. It does not remove links in the devices to which it is linked and is therefore not a substitute for correctly deleting links.

For most SmartLinc switches, factory reset is accomplished by pulling out the set button as far as it will come out until the device powers off and waiting ten seconds, and then pushing it in and holding it for three seconds. After a few seconds, the switch will power on it's controlled load indicating that the factory reset is complete.

Repairing and managing links using HouseLinc

HouseLinc software and a Powerline Controller (PLC) make it easy to correct all of your programmed links at once. Even when you've already installed your system, HouseLinc has the ability to "spider" your network to discover all your INSTEON devices—essentially, it reads the link tables of a few devices you introduce it to and uses those tables to discover the addresses of other devices on your network, and then repeats the process.

Due to the maximum bandwidth of INSTEON over a powerline, using HouseLinc to read the state of all your devices can take upwards of an hour. But once you've done it, you can see and correct your link programming easily with a drag-and-drop interface on your computer. It also takes quite a while to record changes back to the devices.

HouseLinc is easy to use, and I strongly recommend using it for any whole home system.

X-10 troubles

INSTEON devices may be linked together using X-10 group addresses and they sometimes come shipped from the factory this way. You may also be receiving X-10 signals from neighboring houses.

> You can't see X-10 links using HouseLinc or other link programming software—this can keep X-10 link related problems hidden from your troubleshooting actions.

If INSTEON devices are behaving strangely and turning on seemingly randomly, perform a factory reset on the affected devices to clear their X-10 tables and reprogram their links.

Device failure

Device failure is always a possibility with an electronic component—especially components that perform high-power switching. Amongst the 100 or so INSTEON devices in my network, only one has failed and it was my fault.

It is possible for dirty (poorly conditioned) power to cause INSTEON devices to "lock up" or fail to function even though they are powered. Unplug the device, or if it is installed, pull the set button out until the device powers off for ten seconds to reset it.

The troubleshooting hallmark of device failure of course is that the trouble is limited to a single device, irrespective of what the trouble is. If the device seems functional but problematic, perform a factory reset. If the factory reset fails to resolve the problem, swap the device with another equivalent somewhere else in the house. If the problem moves with the device, the device is bad. If the problem remains in place with the new device, the trouble is caused by powerline conditions on the circuit that it is plugged into.

Overloaded Dimmer

Standard INSTEON dimmers are rated for 600 watts. They will easily handle any single incandescent light fixture, but problems arise when you are driving more than one light. The power required is the sum of all the lights on the circuit. You need to sum the wattages of all the lights on a circuit and ensure that they are under the load rating of the dimmer you use to control them.

In my home, I connected a KeypadLinc Dimmer the chandelier without thinking twice about it. Six months later, the light when out and the KeypadLinc was dark with no LEDs lit. When I went to look at it, the device was extremely hot. I pulled out the reset button to "Air gap" the device, and it cooled off. Once cool, I pushed it back in and the device worked, but it still ran very hot.

The problem was that the chandelier has 12 60-watt light bulbs and drew 720 watts, and the KeypadLinc was only rated for 600 watts. After six months of being overloaded, the device had locked up and was now permanently damaged.

The solution was to replace it with a 1000-watt INSTEON dimmer. Unfortunately, there are no 1000-watt KeypadLinc dimmers, so I had to move the KeypadLinc to the next gang in the junction box.

If you have a problem requiring more than 1000 watts, you must use a Relay device. INSTEON relays can handle the full wattage of any 120-volt circuit.

Inductive Loads & Dimmers

Inductive loads are loads such as fans and transformers (used in low-voltage lighting).

There are three ways to reduce the power to an inductive load:
- Using a potentiometer (a variable resistor)
- Using a Variac (a variable transformer)
- Using a variable frequency semiconductor switch

All three methods have problems. Variable resistors convert some of the unused energy to heat, causing considerable heat buildup in the switch.

Variacs don't produce heat, but they are large, hard to find, and comparatively very expensive.

Variable frequency silicon switching is both efficient and inexpensive, but the switching frequency it creates will go in and out of harmonic phase with the induced magnetic field as the switch rate is changed. Out-of-phase switching will cause the magnetic load to vibrate, which in turn can cause very loud buzzing as the motor vibrates against its enclosure or whatever it is mounted to. The vibration can also cause the electrical components to wear out early, so it's important to make sure you tune the dimming to reduce the buzz as much as possible. You might also try shock-mounting the fan or transformer hardware to dampen vibration, but those sorts of measures can get quite expensive and aren't possible in all cases.

INSTEON does not recommend that you use INSTEON dimmers with inductive loads, and I echo that advice with the caveat that if you know what you're doing and you're not too worried about damaging the devices in question, and you don't mind the buzz, you won't cause any ancillary problems. There are no other types of INSTEON dimmers available.

Hot Dimmers

If you are running a considerable load through a Dimmer, the dimmer will get warm. However, it should never get hot to the touch. A dimmer is too hot when the faceplate screws above and below it are obviously hot to the touch.

If you have more than one dimmer in the same junction box, the National Electrical Code requires that you "de-rate" the switches by 20%--in other words, you have to reduce the maximum allowable load on the switch by 20%. This means that a 600W dimmer can only be used to drive a 480W load, and a 1000W dimmer can only be used to drive an 800W load.

A good rule of thumb is to always de-rate the load by 25% for any switch. This way, if someone else installs a higher wattage light bulb there is cushion built into the load calculations.

INSTEON Dimmers that run constantly hot will heat the devices next to them in a junction box and they may fail. You may have to air-gap the switch in order to cool it off, and then replace it.

If you are driving more than one fixture from a single dimmer, you should strongly consider using a 1000W dimmer. If the math comes out to more than 750 watts with the largest bulb someone may use in the fixture, consider going to a relay rather than a dimmer.

1000W dimmers have four "ears" that can be removed. However, these ears are critical to achieving enough heat-sink surface area to dissipate the heat generated when driving a 1000W load. Each of the four ears is dissipates the heat generated by 100W of load, so if you break off two, you've effectively de-rated the dimmer to 800W, and if you break off all four, you'd de-rated it to 600W. Install 1000W dimmers by themselves in a single-gang junction box if possible. If you have to install them in a multiple gang junction box, put them on the left or right side so that you don't have to break off all the heat sink ears.

If you are already running a 1000W dimmer and the switch still runs hot, replace it with a relay. INSTEON relays do not heat up significantly even under full load.

> Look around your house for switches that run more than one fixture. Ceiling cans, Bathroom sconces, chandeliers, and outdoor lights are all places where you have to be careful about total wattage for dimmers.

When you have to call an electrician

Any time you realize that you can't figure out what's going on with an electrical circuit or INSTEON device, call an electrician. It's fairly easy to explain INSTEON to them, and in my experience they're always impressed by it. They can help you determine whether unusual wiring causes the problems you're experiencing or not.

Electrical problems you probably shouldn't attempt to tackle yourself unless you have journeyman electrical experience include:
- Installing a hardwired phase coupler at a circuit breaker
- Installing a powerline filter at the electrical main point of entry
- Installing 30 Amp 220v switches such as the EZSwitch30
- Installing neutrals to switchboxes in older homes

Summary

There are actually not that many problems that can occur with INSTEON below the layer of link programming. INSTEON installations become more reliable the larger they are, and with good phase coupling, you won't run into any trouble beyond the possibility of a failed device.

Chapter 7
Manual Link Programming

Once you have your INSTEON devices installed, it's time to create your links. This chapter is all about creating the links that you planned when you designed your system. There are two ways to create links in an INSTEON system: Manually, and automated link programming with a computer or home automation controller. This chapter covers manual link programming. Chapter 8 covers automated link programming using HouseLinc.

Manual link programming is easy, fast, and uncomplicated. It's perfect for systems that won't change much and for homeowners who want control of their system without learning specialty software, and for changes that you think of and want to implement immediately and easily.

The greatest advantage of INSTEON is the ease with which the owner can create and change the links between devices. Consider a typical centrally controlled or UPB system: The company that installed it for you will have to come out and make all changes you need. You'll pay for at least an hour of programmer labor to make any change. Even homeowner-installed systems such as Z-Wave require centralized change from a centralized controller, although you can do it yourself.

TERMINOLOGY: LINKING

AutoLinc—A feature of HouseLinc that enables walk-through introduction of devices to the software. Using AutoLinc, you can establish your initial list of devices by simply walking around and pressing each switch button for ten seconds.

Cross-link—The state of having two or more devices linked as both controllers and responders of one another. When devices are cross-linked, the state of all devices will be in sync.

Device ID—The INSTEON address of a device. When using HouseLinc, you may need to manually enter device IDs if you do not want to use AutoLinc.

HouseLinc—SmartLabs' PC based link management software. By interfacing your computer with your INSTEON system using a Powerline Modem or Powerline Controller, HouseLinc will allow you to configure links centrally and upload the links you create on the computer into your switches.

Link—Reciprocal link table entries in two devices that allow the controlling device to send commands to the receiving device and receive status responses.

Multi-link—A manual method for linking more than one receiver to a single controller.

On-level—The percentage of full voltage that a dimmer will come on to when the switch is pressed once. In a typical switch, the on level is 100%. In an INSTEON dimmer, the on-level can be custom programmed to any level.

Broken Link—A link that exists only in either the controller or receiver, when no reciprocal entry exists. One-way links will cause various simple malfunctions.

Ramp rate—the time it takes for a dimmer to bring its load to full voltage. Slower ramp-rates appear as gradual increases in light.

Toggle mode—A mode of KeypadLinc buttons that allows a single button to toggle between sending on commands and off commands. In non-toggle mode, a particular button sends only on or off commands, not both.

With INSTEON, you need nothing. You don't need a centralized controller, a computer-based link programmer, or anything else. The devices themselves can establish the links in a way that couldn't possibly be simpler. You have the option to use centralized programming if you'd like, and with complex systems that you want to reconfigure frequently, it's definitely easier to use them—but with INSTEON centralized controllers aren't necessary.

> Linking instructions in this chapter are for SwitchLinc, ToggleLinc, and KeypadLinc switches, because these will be the majority of devices in your network. Other devices are similar.

Creating a link

Manually programming links between INSTEON switches is trivially simple: Press and hold the switch that will be the controller for a few seconds until the LED on the device begins to flash, and then walk over to the responder and press and hold it's switch or set button it flashes as well.

That's it. The switches are linked. The controller will now control the responder.

This creates a single-directional link, meaning that the responder will not change the status of the controller in any way. The controller simply directly controls the responder.

Linked devices will not always be in the same state. For example, the responder may be off, but the controller is on. In order to turn on the responder, you'll have to press the on button even though the controller is already on. Or, if the switch is a KeypadLinc toggle button, you'll have to first turn the button off and then turn it back on in order to turn on the responder.

> If two devices should always be in the same state, cross-link the devices.

Deleting a link

To delete a link in an INSTEON device, press and hold the "on" position switch for ten seconds until it begins to blink. Then, press and hold the switch button again for ten seconds (or the set button for 3 seconds) until the light begins to blink again. Once you've done that, walk over to the device that you wish to unlink and press it's on position switch for ten seconds or it's set button for three seconds. The link between the devices will be removed.

When you create a link, both devices record an entry in their internal link tables. The entry in the responder records the controller's ID code so that it will respond to commands from it, and the controller records the receiver's ID code so that it can receive acknowledgements from it.

Deleting links is problematic because it's very difficult to determine which devices have corresponding links without using HouseLinc software.

Deleting all links

The problem with deleting links in an existing device is that there's really no way to know what links are in it other than manually switching on lights and figuring out what comes up. While you can figure out what devices it controls by using it, there is no simple way to know which devices it responds to unless you've kept scrupulous track of the links you've made (nearly impossible) or you use HouseLinc software.

DELETING ALL LINKS

⇒ Pull the set button all the way out for ten seconds. The device will be unpowered and the LED will go out.

⇒ Push the set button all the way in and hold for three seconds. It's easy to accidentally not get the set button all the way in, or to not hold it long enough, so if the load light doesn't flash, you'll need to start over.

If you want to re-purpose a switch, or if the programming has become confused, you can delete all links by performing a factory reset. A factory reset is also the first troubleshooting step you should perform if you suspect that a device is malfunctioning.

Factory resets are a last resort—not a primary method for repurposing devices. You should manually delete all the links that you know about rather than factory resetting to avoid leaving broken links in linked devices. The only way to remove broken links is to factory reset a device, to re-link it to the same device, or to use HouseLinc to delete the broken link entry.

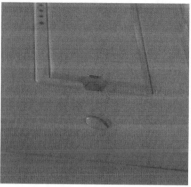

Figure 7.1: A SwitchLinc with the set button pulled out for reset

The "Whole House" factory reset

If your linking has become hopelessly confused due to multiple moves without deletes and you don't want to use HouseLinc to fix it, you may want to consider simply factory resetting all of your devices and reprogramming your links.

It's not as heinous as it sounds—You just walk around to each device, perform the factory reset procedure, and when complete, you have a fresh INSTEON system with no bad links programmed. You can then re-program all the links you intend to have without any side effects.

> While a whole-house factory reset is a last resort, at least it is a resort. You needn't live with badly programmed links forever or be forced into buying HouseLinc to fix them.

Cross-linking

To cross-link them, reverse the order of the devices and link them again. This will cause the devices to control one another in tandem—when one changes state, the other changes to the same state.

Cross-linking is most important with KeypadLinc buttons. If you want the KeypadLinc button to indicate the lit status of the linked switch, you must cross-link it. Otherwise, the button will simply toggle between off and on (by default) and may not indicate the state of the linked switch.

It is not always possible to keep a switch in sync with the state of multiple remote switches, especially when a single button controls more than one switch.

Advanced Manual Programming

INSTEON switches include functionality beyond simple linking, and nearly all of it can be controlled manually. However, it can be difficult to remember advanced programming sequences because you won't use them that often.

The most common advanced manual programming sequences are:
- Setting a custom on-level
- Setting a custom ramp-rate
- Multi-Link Mode

The next sections detail how to set these programming functions in typical SwitchLinc controllers.

Setting a custom on-level

The On-Level is the percentage of full-voltage that a dimmer will come on to when you press the on button. By default, it is 100%, but you can lower it to meet your typical needs.

It's easy to override a custom on-level, either by double-tapping the on switch which will turn the light on to 100% instantly, or by pressing and holding the on switch after turning the light on to bring the light up to 100% from the custom on-level.

SET A CUSTOM ON LEVEL
⇒ Dim the light down to the desired on level.
⇒ Press the set button once (the light will flash)
⇒ Test by pressing the on button
⇒ Wait four minutes before programming any links

Setting a custom ramp-rate

The ramp-rate is the speed at which a dimmer comes to the on level. The slower the speed is, the more dramatic the lighting will appear, at the cost of taking time to turn on. To override the ramp-rate and turn the light 100% on or off quickly, double-tap the button.

SET A CUSTOM RAMP RATE
⇒ With dimmer corresponding to slower, dim the light to the desired ramp rate
⇒ Press the set button twice (the light will flash twice)
⇒ Test by pressing the on button
⇒ Wait four minutes before programming any links

Multi-Link

Multi-Link allows you to set multiple responders to a single controller all at once, without having to create a link for each as a separate step. You simply put the controller into multi-link mode, then walk through to link each responder, and then return to the controller to complete the linking.

Complex cross-linking is considerably easier to perform using HouseLinc.

Multi-Link can also be used to create multiple cross-links. To cross-link more than two devices so that they all track one another's load (such as in a typical three-way or 4-way switch), simply perform the multi-link procedure all the way through for the first switch, the second switch, and all the remaining switches.

LINK MANY RESPONDERS TO A SINGLE CONTROLLER

⇒ On the controller, Press the on button for ten seconds to enter link mode and then press the set button for three seconds to enter scene setup mode. The LED will blink slowly.

⇒ On each receiver, press and hold the on button for ten seconds until the LED blinks, and then press and hold the set button for three seconds. The load on the controller will flash to confirm the linking. Repeat this step for each receiver you want to link to the controller.

⇒ When finished, return to the controller and press the on button to complete the linking process. If at any time more than four minutes passes with no linking activity, the multi-link mode will time out and the controller will exit linking mode.

CROSS-LINK MULTI-WAY SWITCHES

⇒ To cross-link more than two switches, use the procedure "Link Many Responders to a Single Controller" for the first switch.

⇒ Move to the next switch in the group, and considering it as the controller, repeat the procedure all the way through.

When to advance to computer control

Installing and setting up INSTEON is easy. But making changes to programming, swapping devices out, and removing programming from switches is not so easy. The problem is that a device may have a number of links programmed into it, and there's no easy way to tell what they all may be.

HouseLinc, Indigo, and the ISY-99i provide visibility into exactly how a particular device is programmed, as well as the ability to modify that programming.

If you've gotten lost in the programming of your switches because you haven't been able to keep track of all the links in your head or on paper, and you don't want to perform a whole-house factory reset, you should consider using HouseLinc, Indigo, or an ISY-99 to fix your links.

Summary

One of the great advantages of INSTEON technology is the ease with which you can get started. Manual link programming makes getting started easy, and may be the only method you need to use. Nearly everything you will need to do with INSTEON devices, including creating and deleting links as well as advanced programming can be accomplished using manual link programming.

Chapter 8
Link Programming with HouseLinc

Linking becomes increasingly complicated as the number of links and switches in the system increases. With the complications required for multi-way cross-linked switches, manual linking can take quite some time and it can be easy to lose track of where you are in the process.

When linking becomes too complicated, you have a decision to make:
- Purchase HouseLinc and a HouseLinc compatible Powerline Modem, which will enable you to use a Windows PC to manage links
- Purchase Indigo 4 and an Indigo compatible Powerline Controller, which will allow you to use a Macintosh to manage links
- Purchase an ISY-99i and a Powerline Modem, which will allow you to use any computer to manage links.

This chapter details the use of HouseLinc II, SmartLabs' software designed specifically for INSTEON link programming. While there are other applications packages and home automation controllers that can manage INSTEON, these three options are the only ones that are feature complete and reasonably trouble free according to my testing, so they are the only options I can recommend.

TERMINOLOGY: HOUSELINC

Action—A set of INSTEON commands that will be sent when a triggering event occurs and when its associated conditions are met.

AutoLinc—A feature of HouseLinc that allows the software to automatically discover INSTEON devices by walking around and setting them to link mode one after another without returning to the computer.

COM Port—Communications ports are named areas of memory used by software to send codes to a serial device. The INSTEON PLM uses an internal USB to Serial converter, which requires the PLM to be assigned to a COM port in order to take advantage of more reliable software drivers to communicate between the computer and the PLM.

Condition—A filtering condition that can be used to prevent a trigger from sending an action.

Discovery—The process of reading identity information to determine the type of a device and its link table data given only its device ID. HouseLinc uses discovery to inspect the parameters of devices whether they are manually added, found by spidering, or found by AutoLinc.

HouseLinc—Home automation software from SmartLabs that is capable of programming and controlling INSTEON devices from a computer running modern versions of Microsoft Windows.

Powerline Modem—An INSTEON device that interfaces a computer to the INSTEON powerline network. Recent INSTEON PLMs also store and manage events so that a computer need not be attached in order for an event system to run.

Spidering—A technique used to discover INSTEON devices on the network by reading the link tables of known devices, finding IDs of devices that are not yet known to HouseLinc, and then reading their link tables until all devices that have ever been linked on the network are discovered.

Synchronization—A method by which two sets of data are made equal to one another by cross inspection and copying data elements that are missing in either set. In HouseLinc, the HouseLinc software database is kept in synch with the link table in each INSTEON device.

Trigger—An event that stimulates a response. In HouseLinc, Triggers are actions such as a keypad press or time of day that causes the event mechanism in a PLM to wake up and determine whether or not to send commands.

USB—Universal Serial Bus is the interface technology used to connect a computer to a PLM.

Automated link programming requires a computer, software, and an INSTEON Powerline modem or controller to interface the computer to the powerline network. Once you learn how to do it, automated link programming is a powerful tool for creating very sophisticated scenes, for specifying minute details of operation, and for troubleshooting. Large installations or complex installations with a lot of different requirements should strongly consider automated link programming.

Before you purchase a home automation controller or software other than HouseLinc, verify that the system correctly programs INSTEON links rather than just directly controlling devices. If it does not create INSTEON links, you should strongly consider using HouseLinc for link programming to ensure that your system will work if your computer is off or the home automation controller fails.

HouseLinc 2 is the current version as of the time of this writing, and all the instructions in this book refer to HouseLinc 2.

HouseLinc version 2 uses a synchronization paradigm rather than a "read from network, write to network" paradigm used by its predecessor. Most instructions are the same in this book and will work with either version so long as you remember that you will have to manually save changes to the network using the original version of HouseLinc.

HouseLinc operates at the level of INSTEON device links. It does not layer a more sophisticated or abstract device management paradigm such as Scene management, instead keeping its user interface and functionality directly tied to the operations that are directly performed by INSTEON devices—the creation of links. More sophisticated scene management is available in 3rd party software applications and in home automation controllers.

Setting up HouseLinc

To install HouseLinc, you must have a Windows PC running Windows 2000, XP, or Vista, the HouseLinc software, and a Powerline Controller or Powerline Modem compatible with your version of HouseLinc.

To setup HouseLinc, install the software onto your PC, plug the PLM in, and connect the USB cable from the PLM to the PC. Start the software, and perform any requested software upgrades. The process is very simple.

Problems with HouseLinc

I did run into some trouble starting HouseLinc II when I first installed it. When I connected the PLM to my computer, it was automatically assigned a COM (communications) port higher than the COM port of my computer's Bluetooth adapter. HouseLinc inspects COM ports in order to find the PLM, and when it inspected the Bluetooth adapter, HouseLinc would simply crash. This unfortunately meant that it crashed immediately every time I started it, right out of the box.

It took me a considerable amount of troubleshooting to determine what was going wrong, and I am a professional computer technician. I fixed the problem by using the Windows device manager to assign a lower COM port to my INSTEON PLM so that HouseLinc would find it first when it searched for communications devices. If HouseLinc crashes on startup when you first install it, assign the PLM to COM1 and see if that doesn't solve the problem.

Another problem with HouseLinc involves the fact that HouseLinc tends to use most of the bandwidth on your INSTEON network when it's synchronizing devices. This means that when you are using HouseLinc to change things, routine operation of lights and devices will slow down and lights will take longer to come on because of the bandwidth HouseLinc is using.

This bandwidth usage even affects HouseLinc itself—often when you cancel an operation, it can take many minutes in the background for the operation to actually finish. This can make it seem like some of the operations you attempt to perform in the mean time aren't working. The solution is to give HouseLinc a few minutes to "settle" after making changes before doing things like introducing new devices to the network.

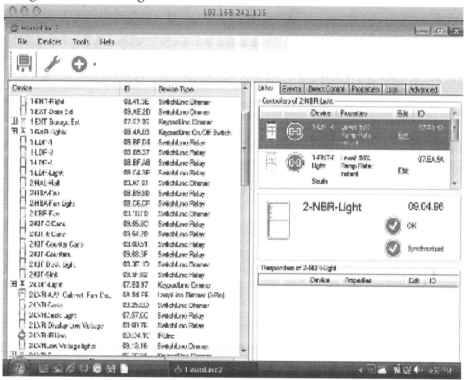

Figure 8.1: The HouseLinc II user interface

Finally, there are occasions (especially after a large amount of network updates, or after cancelling an operation) when the PLM seems to no longer be able to communicate with the HouseLinc software. You can tell when this situation is occurring because the HouseLinc log will show that no devices can be found on the network. This problem is resolvable by exiting HouseLinc, unplugging the PLM from the wall, plugging it back in, and restarting HouseLinc 2.

Managing Devices with HouseLinc

HouseLinc manages your INSTEON devices, so you need to be able to add devices to the HouseLinc database and remove them. You can also use HouseLinc to swap devices, which allows you to replace a malfunctioning device with a matching device and program the new device with all the links that its predecessor had.

There are two ways to enter your devices into HouseLinc:
- Manually enter the INSTEON address of the device
- Use HouseLinc's AutoLinc feature to perform a walk-through "introduction" of all of your INSTEON switches to the PLM that HouseLinc controls.

Of the two methods, AutoLinc is by far the easier. You should use it unless it's simply not feasible to do it.

AutoLinc

To setup HouseLinc using the AutoLinc feature, you simply click "AutoLinc" in the HouseLinc menu and then walk through your home putting each switch in Link mode (usually by holding the "off" position for ten seconds). HouseLinc can then read the device ID from the network and discover what sort of INSTEON device it is. The complete list of devices becomes your initial configuration in HouseLinc once you've completed the walk-through linking.

ADDING DEVICES TO HOUSELINC USING AUTOLINC

SET AUTOLINC MODE
- ⇒ Start HouseLinc
- ⇒ Select Devices -> Add New Device
- ⇒ Click the AutoLinc tab
- ⇒ Click Start

LINK DEVICES

⇒ Go to each device in order, and press the set button for 3 seconds. Alternatively, you can press the switch paddle (off or on) for ten seconds.

⇒ Repeat for each device. When finished, return to the computer and click OK to complete the AutoLink

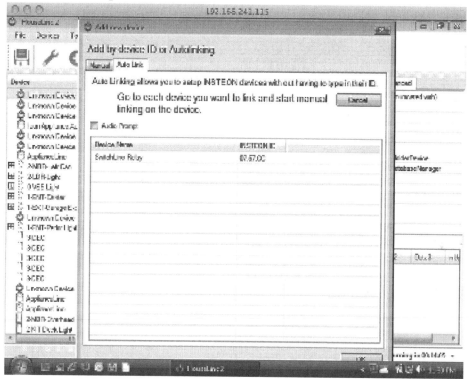

Figure 8.2: HouseLinc in AutoLinc mode

There is a significant problem with AutoLinc: Devices are not given useful names automatically, and you can wind up with a long list of devices in HouseLinc that are not described by their location. You then have to figure out which of the dozens of listed "SwitchLinc Dimmers" control which fixtures. This is a problem in large whole-home installations.

The simplest way to handle this problem is to AutoLinc one room at a time, returning to the computer while the order of switches is fresh in your mind, and then name each switch. This will take more time than a large-scale AutoLinc, but it keeps the order problem manageable.

AutoLinc won't record devices that HouseLinc doesn't have database entries for, and this can throw off your order of entry. If you seem to have a problem with fewer devices listed in the AutoLinc window than you attempted to link, this is probably why. You may need to work back to determine which devices weren't recorded.

If you want to AutoLinc your entire system at once, use your cell phone or a digital camera to take a picture of each device as you perform the walk through AutoLinc. This way, you have a photo for each device in the same time-order as the devices are presented to HouseLinc so you can simply go down the list of devices and name them by looking at the photos.

I take the photo with my finger actually on the off button during the 10 seconds I'm waiting for the link to activate. This way I can take the picture from far enough away to both be in focus and to provide enough context to figure out which switch it is. I download the photos into a folder on my computer called INSTEON devices and named each photo after the device's ID. This makes it easy to find devices in my house when I know the ID, and gives me a reference for programming other controllers. If you accidentally sort the list of devices in HouseLinc and lost the "link order," don't worry: The HouseLinc log will contain all the devices by device ID in the reverse order that you linked them so you can match up the photos to the devices.

On rare occasion, HouseLinc may fail to determine the type of an INSTEON device that it should recognize. In that case, the solution is to record the INSTEON device ID, delete it from HouseLinc, and add it back manually. Battery operated devices such as RemoteLinc have to be woken up in order for HouseLinc to find them correctly.

Searching for Devices

Once you've added a few devices to HouseLinc either manually or using AutoLinc, you can use the Search for Devices to find more.

When you use the search feature, HouseLinc will read the link tables of all the devices it knows about, and add all the addresses it finds in those link tables to its device database. It will then discover those devices and read their link tables, repeating the process until no new devices are found. This is a fast way to find the devices in a network that have existing links. This technique is called "spidering" because it "crawls" the "web" of links to discover devices.

> Spidering will only find devices that are linked to by other devices—it's a great time saver in networks where lots of manually created links exist, but there is no guarantee that spidering will find all of your devices.

SEARCHING FOR NEW DEVICES

⇒ Start HouseLinc
⇒ Add as many devices as you conveniently can using the AutoLinc procedure.
⇒ Select Devices -> Search for New Devices. HouseLinc will examine the link tables of all known devices, and then perform device discovery for each address that is unknown to it.

Manually Entering Devices into HouseLinc

HouseLinc lets you enter devices directly by typing in the device ID. Once you've done that, HouseLinc can inspect the device to determine its type and current configuration. You will have to manually enter the location and a name for the device.

HouseLinc cannot add devices to the device database that cannot be immediately discovered. This is somewhat unfortunate because it does not allow you to pre-populate HouseLinc with devices before they are installed. You must add devices to HouseLinc after they have been installed and are available on the network.

MANUALLY ADDING DEVICES TO HOUSELINC

⇒ Start HouseLinc

⇒ Select Devices -> Add New Device. The Add New Device dialog will appear.

⇒ Type in the INSTEON device ID in the form 00.00.00 that is located on a white sticker attached to the device.

⇒ Click the Detect button. HouseLinc will attempt to find the device on the network. If HouseLinc can find the device, it will discover its device type and add it to the list of INSTEON devices in your house. Otherwise, it will inform you that it cannot find the device and the device will not be added to the device list.

What's in a name?

Now that you've added devices, give some thought to how you will name them. Typically, you'd simply name them after the room and the fixture, such as "Bathroom fan" or "Master bedroom lamp." But how many bathrooms do you have? Should the location be the location of the fixture, or the location of the switch (which aren't always in the same room)? And if it's the fixture, how do you name multi-way switches?

The first problem I ran into was my own inconsistent names for rooms. "Entry" was the same room as "Parlor"—now I have switches with engraved keys that use both terms. Should bedrooms be numbered, named by location, or named by the occupant? It didn't seem like putting people's names on switches was right, so I wound up simply numbering them. Should the second floor outside staircase landing be called "patio," "balcony," or "Back deck"? Sit down with your blue prints and determine the names for each room that won't change and that your spouse agrees with before you etch any keys or name your INSTEON devices, or you'll eventually wind up confusing yourself.

One of the primary problems with the HouseLinc interface is that devices are listed in more or less random order: You can sort them by name, device ID, device type, or location, but for managing devices, it is the location that is most important.

Unfortunately, the location column is not listed as the first column, you cannot move the columns around, and the location column is frequently covered over by the right panel at smaller screen sizes. Even when it is visible, you can't sort by location and then by name.

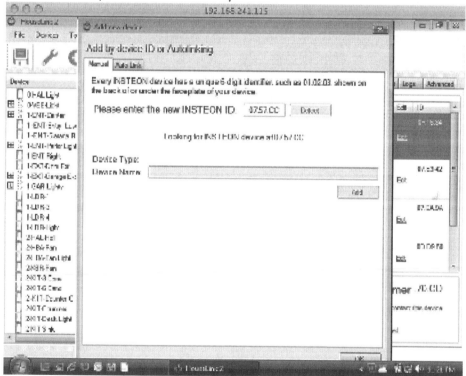

Figure 8.3: Adding a device in HouseLinc

To solve the problem, I name devices using a coded notation that shows the location of the fixture along with the name. This way, when I sort by name, my INSTEON devices are automatically grouped by their floor and room. I can then use the location field to indicate the location of the switch, which is less important and usually just amplifies the location of the switch.

Here are some examples:

- 0-HAL-Light
- 1-GAR-Overhead lighting
- 2-MBR-Right Sconce

In this notation, "0" indicates the basement, "1" indicates the ground floor, and "2" indicates the upper floor. If your house is single story, don't bother with a floor number. HAL is shorthand for Hallway, GAR is Garage, and MBR is master bedroom. I stick to codes of the same length so that the room abbreviations mimic columns in a table.

Make up your own room codes. In my house, I've used the following codes:

- 2BR—Bedroom #2
- ENT—Entry
- EXT—Exterior lighting
- GAR—Garage
- HAL—Hallway
- HBA—Hall Bath
- KIT—Kitchen
- LVR—Living room
- MBR—Master Bedroom
- SYS—System devices whose location is unimportant

I've tried a number of different naming schemes prior to settling on this one, such as including the location of the switch as a code before the name of the fixture, but that didn't turn out to be all that important and it made the names more confusing. I've also tried to put the coded information in the Location field instead of the name field, but then there was no place to put a longhand description of the location, and the location field is frequently hidden.

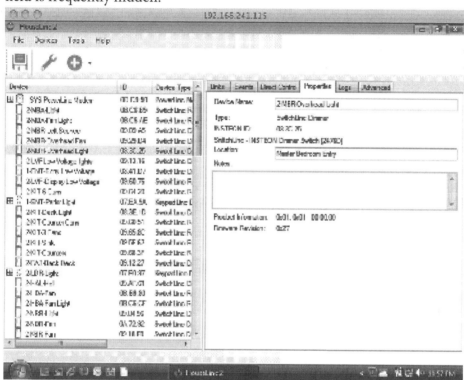

Figure 8.4: Naming Devices

NAMING DEVICES AND SETTING PROPERTIES IN HOUSELINC

⇒ Start HouseLinc
⇒ Select the device that you would like to name in the device list
⇒ In the right panel, click the Properties tab
⇒ In the device name input box, enter the device name
⇒ In the location input box, enter the room in which the device is located

⇒ In the Notes input area, enter amplifying information about the device, such as the exact location of the wall plate or anything not obvious about its programming

Directly controlling devices

HouseLinc can send any supported command to any device that it knows how to manage.

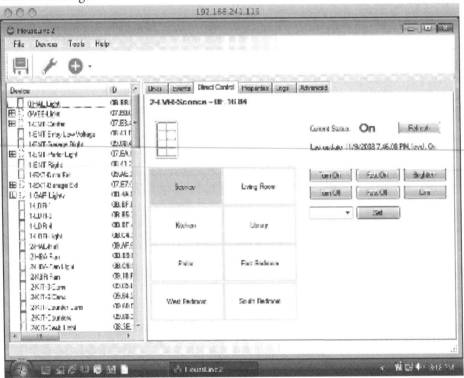

Figure 8.5: Directly controlling devices from HouseLinc

I use HouseLinc direct control primarily for testing. It's great for testing bright levels of various fixtures to determine exactly where you want to set on-levels for various scenes. Different lights and fixtures respond differently to various power level percentages, so the only way to get them working correctly by eye is to actually look at them at the various power levels.

I also go to HouseLinc when I'm at my computer and I realize there's something I'd like to be able to do without getting up. It's my way of finding new uses for INSTEON and prototyping links before I actually program them.

You can actually use HouseLinc as a lightweight central home automation controller, but the user interface isn't designed to be particularly easy to use. For example, HouseLinc does not have an interface for lighting paths or scenes—it can only send commands directly to devices.

Configuring devices using HouseLinc

Devices with specific HouseLinc drivers can have their various options configured by HouseLinc. Primarily, this provides a way to configure the ramp-rate and on-level settings for dimmers and button configuration settings for KeypadLincs.

All devices except KeypadLincs must be manually reset by pulling out their air-gap button for configuration changes made via HouseLinc to take effect.

DIRECTLY CONTROLLING A DEVICE USING HOUSELINC

⇒ Start HouseLinc

⇒ In the device list, select the device you want to control. If the device has multiple buttons or controllers, a "+" button will appear next to the device name. You can click the "+" button to show all the buttons or controllers that the device supports.

⇒ In the right panel, click the direct control tab. The direct control panel will appear showing the various commands that the device can receive.

⇒ Devices that have multiple control buttons will show their various controllers. In this case, click the controller that you would like to directly control.

⇒ In the right panel, click the command that you want to send.

Figure 8.6: Configuring a device using HouseLinc

Deleting a device from HouseLinc

When you take a device out of your network, you have to remove it from HouseLinc. Deleting devices is simple: Select it in the devices control panel, right-click, and select delete.

HouseLinc doesn't just remove the device—it will also remove links to the device from all the linked devices on the network.

DELETING A DEVICE FROM THE HOUSELINC DATABASE

⇒ Start HouseLinc
⇒ In the device list, right click the device you would like to delete and select delete. HouseLinc will remove the device as well as all links to it in other devices.

Swapping out a malfunctioning device using HouseLinc

When INSTEON devices malfunction, replacing the device is the easy part.

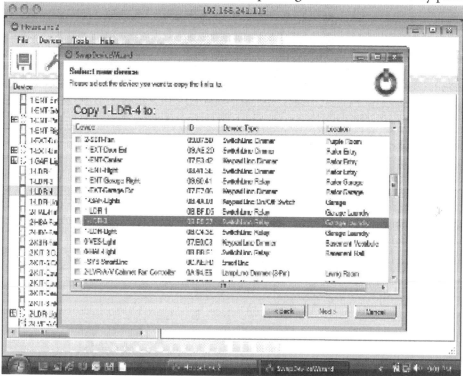

Figure 8.7: Swapping a device using HouseLinc

Re-creating its entire table of links may be quite difficult if it controls a number of devices, as KeypadLincs and other multiple controllers typically do.

There are two modes for swapping operations:
- Switch the link tables of two devices that are on the network
- Replace a device that is no longer on the network with a new device

The mode is automatically determined by whether or not both devices can be found on the network at the same time.

Replacing a device using the swap device feature is easy. Physically replace the old device with the new one so that it is available on the network, add the new device to HouseLinc, then right-click the old device in the HouseLinc device manager and select "swap." The Swap device wizard will appear and will walk you through the process.

SWAPPING A DEVICE USING HOUSELINC

PHYSICALLY CONNECT THE NEW DEVICE TO THE POWERLINE NETWORK

⇒ Using the instructions that came with the device and the procedures in Chapter six, physically install the new device.

⇒ Use either the AutoLinc procedure or the procedure to manually add a device to HouseLinc.

SWAP THE DEVICE

⇒ In the device list, right click on the old device that you want to replace and select swap. The swap device wizard will appear.

⇒ Click Next. Read the note and click next again.

⇒ In the Select New Device list, place a check mark next to the new device in the list and click Next.

⇒ HouseLinc will verify that the devices are compatible and that the new device is communicating on the network. Click Next.

⇒ The device wizard will list three steps that it will perform: Make the new device a responder of all the controllers of the old device, make the new device a controller of all the old devices responders, and delete links to the old device from all devices on the network. If there are any steps that you do not want the wizard to perform, uncheck them.

⇒ Click Finish. HouseLinc will queue all the necessary command and immediately report that it is done. Click OK to close the wizard.

You can use the swap process to copy the link table in a device to a new device without replacing the device. To do this, uncheck the last step in the process when the Wizard confirms which actions you want to take.

Devices HouseLinc cannot manage

HouseLinc doesn't know about or provide any particular extra value for devices such as SmartLinc, IRLinc, EZServe, EZSnsRF, or other whole-network controllers. These devices are either not represented in the device database or there is no specific device configuration driver available, so HouseLinc has only a very limited ability to manage them.

SmartLabs is adding managed devices all the time, so the devices mentioned in this chapter may be supported by the time you read this. Check with SmartLabs for a list of currently programmable devices.

RemoteLinc devices enter a power down state and won't receive commands sent from a HouseLinc unless you manually put them into linking mode before you program them with HouseLinc. The easiest solution is to simply program the HouseLinc manually.

The button tables in HouseLinc are defined in the order that you add infrared buttons to the IRLinc, and they don't reflect naming in HouseLinc that matches them. It's almost certain that this will cause confusion.

The easiest solution is to program the IRLinc manually.

Managing Links with HouseLinc

HouseLinc is designed to make creating and deleting links amongst devices very easy. You can also use HouseLinc to repair broken links and correctly establish cross-links. Finally, HouseLinc automatically acts as a backup device for links in your devices in case they fail and you need to replace the device with another one.

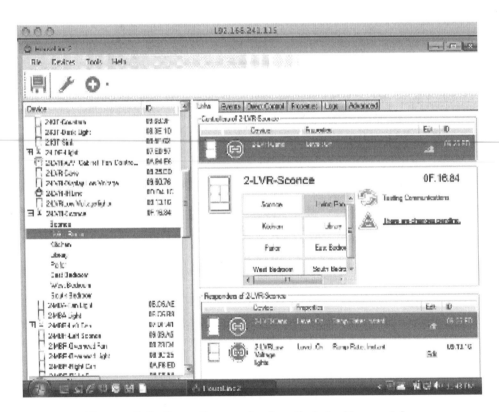

Figure 8.8: Creating a device link in HouseLinc

Creating Links

For most purposes, adding links is easy—simply select the device you want to control or respond to another INSTEON device, and then drag the controller or responder from the device list into the appropriate panel. HouseLinc will automatically create the reciprocal portion of the link in the other device.

Complicated devices have more than one button or controller. For these devices, a "+" symbol will appear next to the device, allowing you to expand the list of buttons. To create links to these buttons, drag the button rather than the device to the controllers' panel of the controlled device.

There are two ways to create a link:

- Select the controller, and drag the responder to the "responders" panel of the controller.
- Select the responder, and drag the controller to the "controllers" panel of the responder.

The two methods are equal opposites, and you can use either method. I generally choose the controller and drag the responder to it, but which method I use depends on how I'm thinking about the problem.

CREATING A DEVICE LINK IN HOUSELINC

CREATING A CONTROLLER LINK

⇒ Start HouseLinc
⇒ In the devices control panel, click the device that will be the controller.
⇒ In the right panel, click the Links tab.
⇒ Scroll the device list to expose the device you want to control.
⇒ Drag the device that you want to control to the lower responders panel in the right panel. HouseLinc will create the link in both devices and synchronize them both.

CREATING A RESPONDER LINK

⇒ In the devices control panel, click the device that will be the responder.
⇒ In the right panel, click the links tab.
⇒ Scroll the device list to expose the device that will be the controller.

⇒ Drag the device that you want to control to the upper controllers panel in the right panel. HouseLinc will create the link in both devices and synchronize them both.

Creating Cross-links

Cross-links allow two devices to control and respond to one another—in other words, when you turn on either device, both devices go on or off.

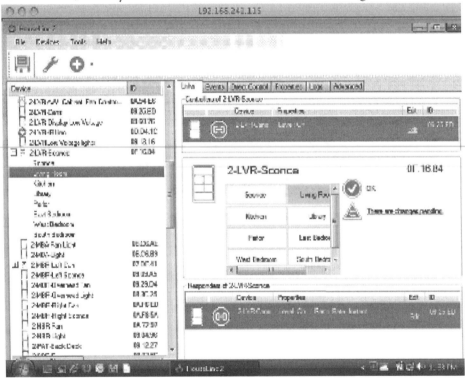

Figure 8.9: Cross-linking two devices in HouseLinc

Cross-links have a related function for multi-function devices like KeypadLincs. The LED that shows the light status is actually a controllable light like any light fixture. Creating a cross link between a fixture and a KeypadLinc button will ensure that the LED in the KeypadLinc accurately reflects the status of the controlled light.

Creating cross-links in HouseLinc is a simple as creating two links: The controller link and its reciprocal responder link. To create a cross-link, drag the linked device to the responders' panel, and then also drag the same device to the controllers' panel. This will establish both reciprocal links in both devices.

If you already have a link in either the controllers or responders panel, you can right-click the link to copy it and then paste it in the opposite panel to create a cross-link.

CROSS-LINKING TWO DEVICES IN HOUSELINC

⇒ Start HouseLinc
⇒ With the first device, create a controller link to the second device
⇒ Right click the created link and select copy
⇒ In the responders panel, right-click on the empty area and click paste. HouseLinc will create a responder link to the same device.
⇒ Double click the link to be switched to the second device. Notice that both controller and responder links to the first device are present.

Deleting Links

Deleting links in HouseLinc is as easy as all the other link management tasks. Just remember to delete the links in both the controllers and the responders panel.

DELETING A LINK USING HOUSELINC

⇒ Start HouseLinc
⇒ Select the device with the link to be removed.
⇒ In the right panel, click the links tab.
⇒ Right click the link you would like to remove and select Delete.
⇒ If you are deleting a cross-link, go to the opposite panel and delete the link to the same device.

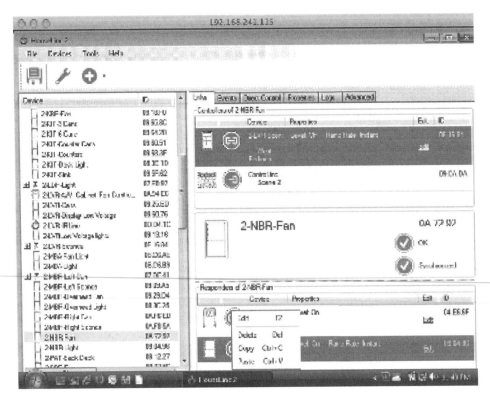

Figure 8.10: Deleting a link

Repairing Links

Every INSTEON link should have an entry in both the controller and the responder. The controller link allows the controller to initially address the responder, and the responder link allows the responder to send feedback to the controller when it completes a command.

Links are "broken" when either a controller or responder link is present but the reciprocal link in the other device is not. HouseLinc flags these links with a "half link" symbol to indicate that you need to decide whether to repair the link or delete it.

Broken links occur when a device is factory reset, when you delete links during time when the opposite device cannot be reached, or if a link creation partially fails for some reason. These occurrences are actually rather common, unfortunately.

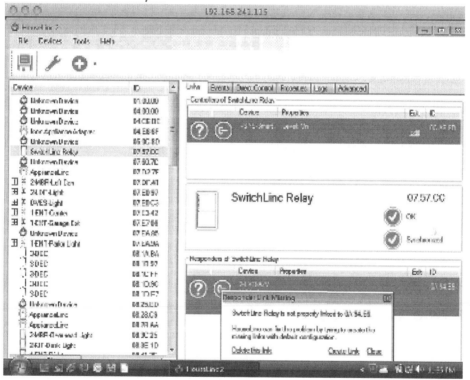

Figure 8.11: Repairing a broken Link in HouseLinc

When a controller link is present but a responder link isn't, the device can be controlled but it cannot report back to the controller its new state, so the controller will flash its LEDs indicating that it received no acknowledgement, and it will attempt to unnecessarily retry the sending the command. When a responder link is present but a controller link is not, nothing will occur—the link simply wastes space in the device link table.

HouseLinc makes it easy to find and repair broken links. Simply click the link and then click either the delete link or create link hyperlinks depending on whether you want to remove or repair the link.

REPAIRING A BROKEN LINK USING HOUSELINC

⇒ Start HouseLinc
⇒ Select the first device in your device list and look for the broken link symbol. Use the down arrow button to scroll through your entire list of devices.
⇒ For each broken link you find, click on the broken link ICON. A popup will appear with two hyperlinks, "Delete Link" and "Create Link." Choose the option appropriate for your scene.
⇒ HouseLinc will queue the commands to repair the link.

Event Management

PowerLinc Modems include more sophisticated microcontrollers than most INSTEON devices, and they have more memory. They also have a real-time clock and programming to determine whether it is light outside based on the programmed latitude and longitude in the device.

HouseLinc can configure the PowerLinc modem to automatically send commands based on time of day information. These are called events, and you can use them to do things like control your INSTEON enabled sprinklers, turn your exterior lights on at night, and turn inside lights off during the day.

> With HouseLinc 2, the events are downloaded into the PLM, so HouseLinc II need not be left running in order for your events to occur. This was not the case with the original version of HouseLinc.

Triggers enable events. Triggering events can times of day, an INSTEON controller button pressed (or pressed twice—a trick you can use to explicitly trigger events), or an X10 device controller event.

Conditions add additional parameters that the PLM will check before sending the event actions. You can use conditions to enable actions only on specific dates, times, or days of the week. Currently, conditions are only time of day or date based, but additional conditions such as the state of other INSTEON devices may be available in the future.

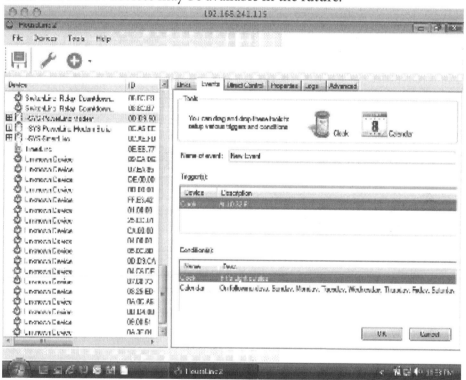

Figure 8.12: Managing Events

To understand the difference between Triggers and Conditions, think of triggers as "actions that wake up the PLM event controller" and conditions as "conditions the PLM event controller checks before it sends commands."

Actions are INSTEON responder links—they indicate the INSTEON device and command you want sent at the specified time.

CREATE AN EVENT TO TURN ON A DEVICE AT SPECIFIC TIMES

⇒ Start HouseLinc
⇒ Click the Events tab
⇒ Drag the clock symbol into the conditions panel
⇒ Click the Edit link on the clock condition
⇒ Select time range in the condition pick list
⇒ Enter a time range such as between 6:00 p.m. and 11:00 p.m.
⇒ Drag the calendar ICON to the conditions panel
⇒ Click Edit on the calendar condition
⇒ Uncheck Saturday and Sunday in the calendar panel
⇒ Drag the devices you would like to control, such as exterior lights, to the Actions panel.
⇒ Click save. At the indicated days and times, the selected devices will come on.

Troubleshooting with HouseLinc

HouseLinc is a fantastic troubleshooting tool. It has the ability to test and log attempts at communication amongst all the devices on your network.

The troubleshooting capabilities of HouseLinc include:
- Manually re-synchronizing devices
- Displaying low-level device information and advanced properties
- Displaying logs of all HouseLinc activity
- Running diagnostic communications to determine packet loss

Combined with your map of device locations, HouseLinc can make it simple to determine when you have a wiring problem, an appliance that may be absorbing signals, or a problem with your phase coupling.

Setting up a troubleshooting station

One of the first problems I ran into while installing devices (especially KeypadLincs) was simply running back and forth between my computer running HouseLinc and the installed device that I was troubleshooting.

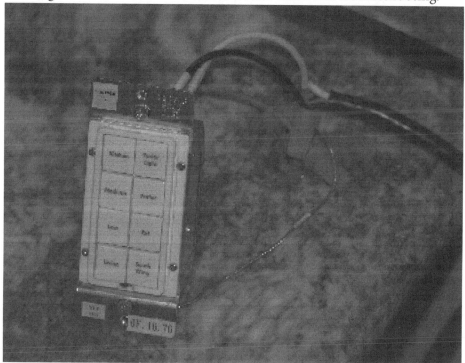

Figure 8.13: Setting up a KeypadLinc before installation

The simple solution is to move the INSTEON device near my computer by wiring the device to a three-prong power cord using wirenuts. Then I can simply plug in the INSTEON device to a nearby outlet and perform the installation link programming at my desk. Once the device programming works correctly, I unwire it from the cord and install it permanently.

> If you wire an INSTEON device to a power cord, be absolutely certain that the HOT and NEUTRAL wires have no exposed wire at all after the wirenut is attached. INSTEON devices can be safely used on a test bench as long as no wires are exposed.

I bought a power cable with tinned ends that I use to connect INSTEON devices to the outlet next to my computer. If you purchase a cable (rather than cutting an existing one) the ends will be tinned and the wires will be black, white, and green corresponding to hot, neutral, and ground. Your mileage will vary if you cut your own.

Requesting a Synchronization

When you make a manual change to an INSTEON device, that change won't be reflected in HouseLinc until the routine daily maintenance operation has occurred. If you don't normally leave HouseLinc running, this maintenance operation will occur when you start HouseLinc.

If you want a manual change you've just made to be immediately reflected in HouseLinc, you can request synchronization. This will cause HouseLinc to read the device's link table and update the HouseLinc device database to reflect those changes immediately.

RE-SYNCHRONIZING A DEVICE

⇒ Start HouseLinc
⇒ Right-click on the name of the device you would like to re-synchronize
⇒ Select Synchronize. HouseLinc II will re-synchronize with the device and read any new device links from the device link table. If an unknown device is discovered in the link table, HouseLinc will attempt to discover that device.

Reading Logs

HouseLinc creates a log of all of its activities that you can use to troubleshoot problems and determine what HouseLinc is doing behind the scenes.

Here are some examples of typical log entries:

11/22/2008 7:05:24 PM   NOTICE   2-LVR-IRLinc   Status
update: device was responding.

11/22/2008 7:05:41 PM   INFO Updating properties for 2-LVR-
IRLinc 0D.D4.1C

11/22/2008 7:12:35 PM   WARN Resetting database read for
0C.AE.FD, looks like the database was changed since last
read

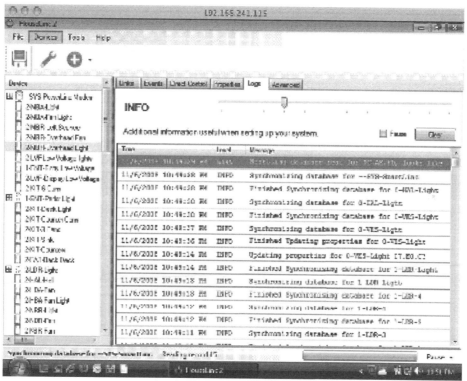

Figure 8.14: The HouseLinc communications log

Log entries are useful for determining such things as the exact order that AutoLinc devices were discovered, error messages relating to device that should be reachable but aren't, and indications that the PLM might be malfunctioning.

ADDING DEVICES TO HOUSELINC USING AUTOLINC

⇒ Start HouseLinc.

⇒ Click the Logs tab in the right panel. Scroll down through the log to examine actions HouseLinc has taken on the network.

Examining advanced device options

Advanced device options show information about the selected device such as its exact type and its revision number, as well as the raw database link table. I've used the Advance options tab to determine why HouseLinc did not recognize SwitchLinc Timers and update the XML database to correctly identify them prior to a HouseLinc update that fixed the problem.

Figure 8.15: Device Advanced Properties

MANAGING DEVICE OPTIONS USING HOUSELINC

⇒ Start HouseLinc

⇒ Select the device whose properties you want to examine in the device list

⇒ Click the Advanced tab

⇒ Scroll through the device properties and the raw link table data.

HouseLinc Diagnostics

The HouseLinc Diagnostic function is a powerful tool for characterizing the quality of your HouseLinc network and your underlying electrical circuits. It does this by methodically communicating with each device on your network repeatedly, and recording how successful the communication attempts are.

The HouseLinc diagnostic screen is simple to use, but can be somewhat difficult to read. The important number to watch is the SD%, which counts the success rate of standard packet transmission.

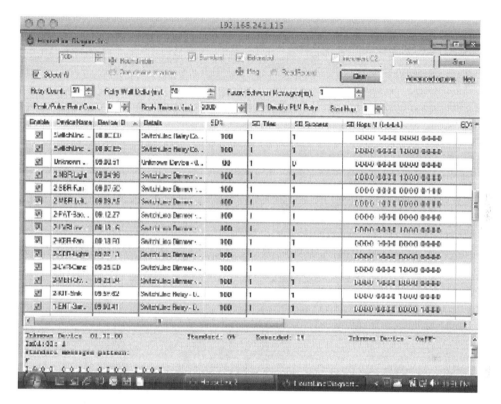

Figure 8.16: The HouseLinc Diagnostics Screen

FINDING PHYSICAL NETWORK PROBLEMS USING HOUSELINC DIAGNOSTICS

RUN DIAGNOSTICS

⇒ Start HouseLinc

⇒ Select Tools -> Diagnostics. The Diagnostics screen appears.

⇒ Click start.

Interpret Diagnostic Information

⇒ Examine the diagnostic information device by device, looking for those devices that have an SD% rating of less than 100% success rate in receiving INSTEON packets.

⇒ Comparing the devices with a low success rate to your blueprints, trying to determine if the devices with little success are distant from other devices, whether they are on the same circuit, whether the device may be on the same circuit as a power strip that may be filtering signals, or what the devices that are missing packets may have in common. Your intuition will guide your troubleshooting.

Summary

HouseLinc makes it easy to manage all of your INSTEON devices in a coherent way and to change their configuration easily and without guesswork. Creating sophisticated scenes, reprogramming complex devices such as KeypadLincs, and deleting old links is far easier for large installations with HouseLinc than manual link programming. HouseLinc also allows you to program a PLM to provide sophisticated scene management.

HouseLinc is invaluable for complex troubleshooting because it can repair broken links, create cross-links easily, remove orphaned links, and perform sophisticated repairs such as swapping failed devices with their link tables in tact. Its diagnostic feature allows you to profile your electrical network to pinpoint physical problems and problem appliances on your network that may require filters or additional INSTEON devices to amplify signals.

Chapter 9
Integrating INSTEON

One of the greatest features of INSTEON is the wide range of options you have for controlling your home automation system. Of all home automation technologies, only X10 has a wider range of integrated software and devices available.

Protocol interfaces such as Powerline Modems, the ISY-99, and EZBridge provide developers with simple ways to interface their systems to the INSTEON network without having to develop electronics. This ease of development translates into an ever-increasing range of devices and technologies that integrate seamlessly with INSTEON.

This chapter covers INSTEON specific web controllers, touch screens, security panels and devices, and computer software that will allow you to control your INSTEON devices any way you want to.

A word about Home Automation Controllers

Home automation controllers are dedicated PCs that run dedicated software and interface with home control technologies such as INSTEON. They usually provide a television output to integrate home control with your universal remote, and additionally can usually receive input from and control touch-screen LCDs and other keypad devices that are typically placed near major doorways.

I've avoided covering dedicated home automation controllers for a number of reasons:

- This book is focused on INSTEON technology, and most home automation controllers are not. They usually have simply tacked on INSTEON support and do not manage INSTEON links. This fails to make use of INSTEON's greatest strength—its decentralized reliability.
- I fundamentally disagree with the idea that home automation is most conveniently controlled by a universal remote or a complex touch screen menu system. I believe that light switches all around the house most effectively control lights, occasionally supplemented by a remote or a touch screen for sophisticated scene management.
- There are a large number of home automation controllers—it is not possible to cover them all.
- They cost vastly more than they're worth in my opinion (more than all your INSTEON devices combined), which goes against another of INSTEON's great strengths.
- They are simply PCs that will eventually fail due to fans or hard disks wearing out, which guarantees that you will eventually have a home automation outage if you rely on them.
- You can easily make one yourself by purchasing a $400 notebook PC, configuring it not to go to sleep, installing your favorite home automation application, and connecting it to a PLM or PLC. And this home automation controller will have a console directly attached to it for troubleshooting purposes.

You can find a wealth of information about home automation controllers on the Internet. They do have strengths in integrating different home automation technologies and can bridge INSTEON commands to Z-Wave devices, for example. If you have numerous different home automation technologies, there may be no solution other than a home automation controller.

The right way to Integrate

The ability of a system to continue to operate when components fail is called fault tolerance. Graceful degradation describes the ability of a system to provide reduced functionality even in the face of significant failure.

There are three major contributing factors to fault tolerance:
- Inherency: At the most basic level, components are capable of safe operation even when failure occurs. Basic functionality is inherent in the design of a component in such a way that it cannot fail.
- Decentralization: No single point of failure can prevent the system from functioning. Failures involve only the loss of function of the failed component itself, not loss of system-wide functionality.
- Layers of operation: Low-level functionality is provided by simple components that are unlikely to fail, while high-level functionality is provided by complex systems that are more likely to fail. The failure of complex components only impacts specific high-level functionality and does not interrupt simpler functions.

It is unlikely that you've ever heard of a standard light switch failing to operate. Light switches that are eighty years old continue to function safely and correctly—because their operation is inherent, the only possible failure is mechanical wear. INSTEON switches don't reach this level of inherency, although with a built-to-purpose relay design that allowed for mechanical actuation, they actually could. But they do fail safely: No matter what happens to an INSTEON switch, pulling out its "air-gap" switch will disconnect power to the switch and circuit safely. This inherent safety prevents INSTEON switches from becoming "stuck on" or unsafe to work on no matter how they've failed.

INSTEON devices are completely decentralized. The failure of any single INSTEON device isn't going to affect any other devices on the network. The web of links between devices does not depend on any central device to function.

A well-designed INSTEON installation is stratified into layers of operation. The first layer is INSTEON switches themselves: They continue to control their local load even if they cannot communicate on the network.

The next layer is group programming. You can program scenes into an INSTEON device as a group, and trigger that scene using a mechanical button.

The next layer up consists of complex devices such as security systems, touch screens, and web controllers. When these devices are configured to activate groups rather than directly controlling individual devices, you aren't relying on them for major functionality—only for convenience.

If you have programmed your groups into an INSTEON KeypadLinc and then configured a Touch Screen system to activate that button (group), then when the touch screen system fails you can still activate the scene using the INSTEON KeypadLinc. Furthermore, you can activate that same group code from multiple complex devices, saving you from having to define the same group separately in numerous devices and allowing you to make changes only to that one device's group in order to change the group throughout all of your complex devices. Finally, you'll have a physical indicator (the KeypadLinc button's LED) that tells you when the group is active.

Contrast this to a home automation controller that directly controls all the INSTEON devices rather than programming groups: When the automation controller fails, your group and scene controls all fail with it.

No matter which of these integration technologies you use, make use of group codes in devices such as KeypadLincs to create and control scenes and use your more complex devices to trigger the groups you program into them, rather than directly controlling numerous lights. This way, you'll always have manual control of scenes when you can't get your more complex systems working.

It is not much harder, nor more much more expensive, to integrate the right way. But you can use a slow-growth approach to building your system that will spread the costs out over time and ensure that you know how your system works before you proceed to the next level. You'll have far fewer frustrations and a system that everyone in your house understands when you design for fault tolerance and graceful degradation.

Web Controllers

The simplest thing you can do to interface your INSTEON network with a computer, web-pad, or cell phone is to use a low-cost web controller. Web controllers are special purpose micro-servers that provide a web page you can use to control your INSTEON devices.

There are three devices currently in the low cost micro-server market for INSTEON:

- The SmartLabs SmartLinc web controller
- The SimpleHomeNet EZServe web controller
- The Universal Devices web home automation controller

I've ordered this list by cost, complexity, and capability—Of the three, the SmartLabs SmartLinc is based on the simplest microcontroller. The SimpleHomeNet EZSrve web controller is based on a capable microcontroller that could be upgradable to perform functions well beyond its current utility, and the Universal Devices ISY-99i is essentially an entire computer in a tiny box that could be upgraded to perform tasks of nearly any complexity.

All of these devices require some level of existing home network infrastructure, including a home computer and a home network of some type, which could be as simple as a single wired or wireless cable/DSL router. You'll usually want to have a broadband Internet connection as well, whether or not you enable access from the Internet so that the device can receive the current time from the Internet.

SmartLinc

SmartLinc is a simple web-based INSTEON controller that integrates a microcontroller and Ethernet adapter with an INSTEON PLM to create a plug-in web-interface for your INSTEON system. The SmartLinc web interface was specifically designed to fit the form factor of the Apple iPhone or iPod Touch, which provides a very low cost "web pad" that you can use with the SmartLinc as a universal remote for your INSTEON system. That said, the SmartLinc would work with any computer or cell-phone that has a web browser, and you can update the firmware with a more basic display that will work well on any phone or computer.

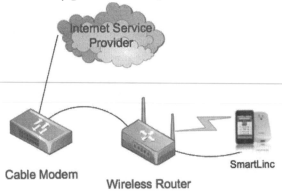

Figure 9.1: Network Diagram for INSTEON Web Controllers

SmartLinc requires that you have an Ethernet network, and it is most effective if you also have a wireless WiFi network. You don't need a broadband Internet connection unless you want to be able to control you INSTEON network from outside your house (but nearly everyone with the required equipment also has broadband Internet).

Be exceptionally careful about exposing your web controller to the public Internet. If your web controller can be remotely accessed, your home can be remotely controlled.

Figure 9.2: SmartLinc Web Interface

Configuring the SmartLinc is easy and can be performed entirely through the web. To get started, you simply plug the SmartLinc into an outlet and your Ethernet switch, and point a web browser at the IP address assigned to it.

SmartLinc can only directly control devices—it does not create or maintain links or perform any sort of link management. This also means, for example, that it does not know whether or not a light is currently on. It merely provides a button pad to directly control lights and presumes that you either know or don't care what the current state of the light is.

That said, in terms of out-of-the-box functionality as of the time of this writing, the SmartLinc is the most focused, easiest to use, and (in my opinion) useful of the three devices—it's capabilities are well tuned to its current purpose, and its low cost reflects that.

Although I own all three of these devices, the only one I routinely use is the SmartLinc—it works well, links to all my devices, and is fast and easy to use.

> One significant problem with the SmartLinc is that it cannot receive the current time from the Internet, and its internal clock is quite inaccurate. Mine has drifted about 30 minutes in six months, and must be reset manually.

EZSrve

EZSrve from SimpleHomeNet was the first all-in-one web interface specifically designed for INSTEON. It has exactly the same form-factor as the SmartLinc interface, but is based on a more sophisticated internal computer. That said, its web interface is not quite as well designed—it was designed for web browsers on general-purpose computers rather than for a specific handheld phone. The website requires a screen too large to be easy to use on a smartphone.

Unlike the SmartLinc, the EZSrve is capable of acting as a network bridge for software running on general purpose PCs or potentially on smartphones to provide the capability for any software application to control INSTEON devices—you can even send commands directly from the command line of your computer if like typing in XML syntax. For example, if you are a programmer or network integrator you could trivially write a script in Perl, Bash, C, Visual BASIC, Python, or any other programming language that can create an HTTP connection to an XML service in order to control any INSTEON device on your network. EZSrve is intended to provide a bridge interface to arbitrary software applications as well as a web interface, and this capability distinguishes it from the SmartLinc.

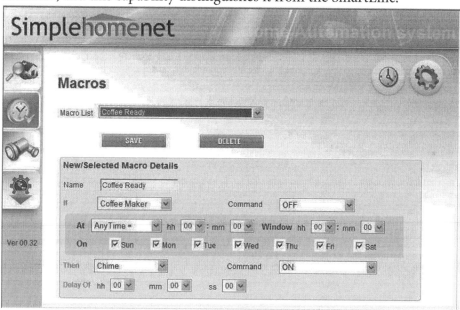

Figure 9.3: SimpleHomeNet EZSrve Web Interface

EZSrve also has event management capabilities and an internal clock with time-of-day triggers, which allow you to perform more sophisticated scene management. Because it can be directly linked with INSTEON devices, it is capable of receiving triggering inputs from INSTEON devices and monitoring the status of devices over the network.

At the time of this writing, SimpleHomeNet is planning to release a free upgrade to the EZSrve that will deliver a far more capable user interface based on Flash web technology. This will allow users to create scenes using sophisticated drag-and-drop commands through a computer's web browser. The Flash user interface will run on PC, Mac, and Linux computers but wil not run on smartphones such as the iPhone, which lack support for Flash technology.

There is a native iPhone App for the EZSrve called XML Remote. It costs $5 and allows you to configure complex scenes using the EZSrve XML dialect. The application is somewhat difficult to setup because you have to construct the XML commands yourself on the phone. Once configured, the app is much faster to respond than the SmartLinc iPhone interface because it is a native application, not a web app. XML Remote can technically control any device that can be controlled via XML, but it comes with built-in support for the EZSrve.

The SimpleHomeNet EZBridge is an earlier device based on similar hardware that provided a web service designed to receive commands over the network from software running on computers and home controllers. Some versions of the EZBridge can be software updated to become EZSrve devices, but all are obsolete as of this writing.

mControl home automation software can use the EZSrve or EZBridge devices to send and receive INSTEON commands, which means that your computer does not need to be located near your PLM or PLC.

Universal Devices ISY-99i IP Bridge/Controller

Universal Devices makes a line of small network servers that are compatible with INSTEON, UPB, and Z-Wave. These devices deliver a Java-based user interface through a web browser that allow you to directly control your home automation devices.

> Universal Devices provided an ISY-99i for testing purposes for this book.

The ISY-99i is a true home automation controller in a tiny package—it is actually a complete computer, and even has a user-upgradable camera-card flash storage card inside it. It combines the features of a web controller, a home-automation controller, a link manager, an Ethernet-to-INSTEON bridge, and an Infrared interface (which is an option).

The scope of the ISY-99i is quite broad and directly comparable to HouseLinc or a home automation controller rather than to a simple web interface designed for direct control like the ones provided by the SmartLinc and the EZSrve (Although it does provide a simple direct control web page). The ISY-99i programs links into INSTEON devices directly, so their scenes will continue to function correctly if the Universal Devices controller is off-line. The ISY-99i stakes out the middle ground between the high cost home automation controller and the low capability web controller.

Because the ISY-99i is a more powerful general-purpose device, it is not as easy to use or setup as the SmartLinc or EZSrve. As a fully-fledged scene manager, it also takes considerable time to add all your devices to the ISY-99. The user interface is complex compared to the direct-control web interfaces provided by the EZSrve and the SmartLinc controllers. It also costs two to three times as much, is considerably larger, and requires an external PLM.

The capability provided by the ISY-99i more than makes up for the complexity of its configuration, and the ISY-99i integrates with a number of other systems to make control easy. Although Java support is required for administration and link management, you can control your lighting from any device that can display a web page, such as the iPhone or any other modern smartphone.

Complex user interface

The user interface of the ISY-99i administrative console is dominated by the choice to use Java for the administrative console. Java is a cross-platform programming language that allows the ISY-99i user interface to run on Windows, Macintosh, Unix, and Linux platforms. It is the only reasonable choice to achieve this cross-platform capability.

When you browse to the address of the ISY-99i, you're presented with a simple, no frills website that will function on literally any web browsing device. This is a benefit compared to the EZSrve, which has a too much interface clutter to function on small displays. You can directly control any device or scene from the web interface, and you can launch the Java administrative interface.

The Java interface applet pops out of the web page and appears in a separate window as if it were a local application. The web browser window that the applet pops out of must remain open, and if you have it selected and accidentally press backspace, you will lose your connection to the controller.

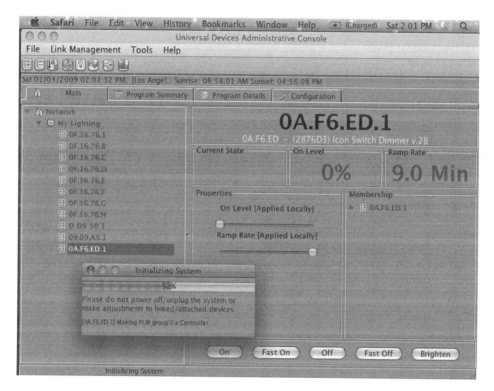

Figure 9.4: Universal Devices ISY-99 User Interface

The user interface is divided into a tree browser that allows you to select device and scenes in the left panel, and details about the selected device or scene in the right panel—fairly typical of computer applications. When you select a device, you can modify the device's options and parameters directly. When you select a scene, you can view the devices in the scene and control the scene-specific on-levels and ramp-rates.

Adding devices to scenes isn't necessarily intuitive—you have to drag the device from the device selection tree to the scene in the same tree. When the list of devices and scenes is longer than the screen will show, it's difficult to make the devices scroll to the correct scene.

The user interface could be more intuitive. Firstly, devices and scenes are merged into the same tree. They aren't the same concept and should be in two separate trees, with the left panel split into a top panel for devices and a bottom panel for scenes. Doing this would make dragging devices into scenes much easier. The length of the device list is exacerbated by the fact that devices with multiple buttons (groups) show up as multiple devices—one for each button or group code the device has. This artifact means that you have to rename each button of a KeypadLinc separately and that if you name them differently, they won't sort next to one another. Group codes should be shown as a sub-tree under the parent device.

The more intuitive mechanism would have been to click the scene, allow it to occupy the right panel, and then drag the devices from the selection tree into the right panel occupied by the scene. Perhaps a software update will make adding devices to scenes easier in the future.

Scene Management

The ISY-99 shines in programming and configuration of your link network. It provides drag-and-drop control of link programming across all the devices in your network. The ISY-99i goes beyond the capability of HouseLinc by providing true Scene Management as well.

HouseLinc provides Group Management—Essentially, you can define all the devices that will respond to a particular controller button. The set of responders of a particular controller (including the controller) is called a Group.

Scenes are similar to groups, but they can have more than one controller. For example, if you have a SwitchLinc next to your front door configured to control your living room cans, lamps, and sconces as a group, with Scene management you could also add the controller switches by your kitchen and hallway to control the same set of responders, and manage the entire set of devices as a scene. Scene Management requires a software program to sort the scene definition into a set of links and cross-links to be programmed into devices, and this is what the ISY-99i does.

Sophisticated Programmed Response

The ISY-99i includes an embedded programming language similar to BASIC that allows you to create complex behaviors, such as requiring a specific time-of-day, trigger, and conditions of multiple INSTEON devices before sending an event. For example, if you have a motion sensor that you would like to trigger a light only after 6:00 p.m. and only when your living room lights are already off, you need a device like the ISY-99i. INSTEON link management and PLM events cannot control events of this sophistication.

Support for complex INSTEON devices

As of the time of this writing, the ISY-99i has better support for the IRLinc, the EZSnsRF, and the EZX10RF than HouseLinc has. These INSTEON devices are complex because they have to be linked to an INSTEON device and a native device at the same time, and linking them using nothing but the set button that comes with them is not simple. The ISY-99i walks you through the process.

Integration with other devices

The ISY-99i provides easy-to-use integration with other home automation equipment such as:
- Elk M1 Gold Security Alarm Panel
- IES Touch Screen INSTEON controller
- Nokia 800/810 Web Pads via InterfaceGO software.
- IES EasyTouch-P Touch Screen

Integration Elk Security alarm panel

The Universal Devices controller is also designed to integrate with the Elk M1 Gold alarm panel, allowing you to enable and disable the alarm system through its web interface and allowing you to control sophisticated scenes built in the Universal Devices controller from Elk alarm system keypads.

IES EasyTouch-P Touch Screen Controller for INSTEON

The IES EasyTouch-P touch screen Controller for INSTEON receives its programming for scenes and devices automatically from the ISY-99i with no configuration, providing a full-color high-end graphical touch screen that can be mounted in walls near entryways or used as a tabletop controller. The Power-over-Ethernet version of the IES EasyTouch requires an ISY-99i as its bridge from the Ethernet network to the INSTEON network.

InterfaceGO Nokia 810 Touch Screen controller software for ISY-99

InterfaceGO makes a software image for the Nokia 810 Web pad that converts it into a home automation touch screen interface for the ISY-99. The system looks much like very high-end home automation controllers, but costs a fraction of the price even when you include all the necessary components:

- Universal Devices ISY-99i web controller
- INSTEON Powerline Modem
- Nokia 800 or 810 Web Pad
- InterfaceGO software image
- WiFi Wireless Access Point

The sum of these components is about $1000, which is still less expensive than the next closest dedicated home automation controller and a fraction of what most home automation controllers cost.

Being a native application on the Nokia means that the software interface is smoother and "Glitch free" compared to web apps, which have at the very least some latency when switching between screens and generally have noticeable artifacts, not the least of which is the visible web browser on the display screen.

IES EasyTouch Touch Screen

IES makes a version of their Touch Screen Interface that is designed to connect directly to your wired Ethernet network and interface with your INSTEON network via the ISY-99i. If you've already got an ISY-99i, you can use this version to avoid purchasing a PLM and locating your Touch Screen near a plug-in outlet.

Summary of the ISY-99i

In sum, the ISY-99i is a true home automation controller. It is by far the best of the bunch for INSTEON control despite its low cost. It can replace a home automation controller, a SmartLinc, HouseLinc or other PC-based home automation software, and an IRLinc (with the optional IR module). Furthermore, it is cross platform providing the same benefits to Windows, Macintosh, and Linux users.

More importantly, it's clear that the people at Universal Devices are real programmers who love to write code, not just people whose job it is to program. It is free from the software defects and poor design decisions that seem to plague home automation software and controllers.

You should strongly consider the ISY-99i as your single home-automation solution. It is superior to more complex home automation controllers for INSTEON utility, comparable to HouseLinc for link management, provides a simple web interface for home automation control, and integrates well with other devices.

Touch Screens

Smarthome systems are strongly associated with touch screens in the minds of consumers. I'm personally not sold on the concept of tapping through a series of menus to control lights or scenes, but there is something to be said for a system that anyone can look at and figure out. The problem with light switches alone is that they don't really tell you what they're going to do. My wife really liked using a touch screen because she didn't have to figure out how I programmed switches—she could read through the touch screen scenes and tell exactly what was going to happen. Removing the mystery from your Smarthome is a big part of making it useful for others, and well designed touch screens can help.

> People who are unfamiliar with your home automation system will probably have an easier time controlling lights via a well-designed touch-screen interface than by using a remote control or flipping light switches to try to figure out what's going on.

Touch screens are relatively expensive propositions in an INSTEON network, but there are some clever options that don't cost nearly as much as the touch screens designed to work with home automation controllers and centralized lighting systems.

The INSTEON-specific ways to incorporate touch screen controllers are:
- Use an iPod Touch, WiFi, and a SmartLinc Web Controller ($450)
- Use an IES EasyTouch-S and a PLM ($600)
- Use an ISY-99, InterfaceGo, Nokia 810, and WiFi ($1000)
- Use an IES EasyTouch-P, an ISY-99, and a PoE Ethernet hub ($1000)

Of these options, only the EasyTouch is available in an in-wall mountable unit that can be permanently dedicated to the control of your INSTEON system. They're also available in a tabletop enclosure for placement on nightstands, counters, and coffee tables.

Because the SmartLinc and ISY-99i options are covered in other parts of this chapter, only the EasyTouch is covered in this section.

IES EasyTouch

There's only one touch screen made specifically for INSTEON at the time of this writing: The IES EasyTouch.

Figure 9.5: IES EasyTouch touch screen

IES makes two versions of what is essentially the same device:

- The EasyTouch-S, which communicates and is powered via an INSTEON 2412S PLM.
- The EasyTouch-P, which communicates and is powered via Ethernet and requires an ISY-99i as a bridge to INSTEON.

Both cost around $500 at the time of this writing. The choice of which touch screen model to purchase is simple: If you have an Ethernet network wired throughout your home and you already have or intend to buy an ISY-99i, use the EasyTouch-P. Otherwise, use the EasyTouch-S. Both models also come as in-wall or tabletop models.

IES provided each model of their touch screen for testing purposes for this book.

From a physical standpoint, the devices are beautifully made. The screen functionality is excellent: the display is bright and the touch panel works perfectly with no need for calibration out of the box. Because the device is powered either by the PLM or by your Power-over-Ethernet hub (depending on which type you purchase) there's no need to run anything but a Category 5 network cable to the point of installation. The in-wall units are designed to be installed into a dual-gang junction box, and the bezel is magnetically attached so it's easy to get off but stays in place securely. The bezels come in white and black, and can be painted to match your décor. The default on-screen graphics are simple without being amateurish and do the job quite nicely.

The EasyTouch-S does not use group commands to activate scenes, so lights come on one-at-a-time in order and may take a few seconds to complete activate in large scenes. Solve this problem by programming a group in another device, such as a KeypadLinc, and then activating that group with the EasyTouch-S. The EasyTouch-P uses ISY-99i Groups.

Configuring the EasyTouch-P

There is no configuration required for the EasyTouch-P. When you plug it into your Ethernet network, it will power on, boot up, find the ISY-99i automatically, and download all the scenes and devices you've configured in the ISY-99i in the space of about twenty seconds. The touch screen is then ready to go. If you make a change in the ISY-99i, simply press and hold the

IES icon in the welcome screen to enter setup mode and press the update button. That's really all there is to it.

If you've changed the password on your ISY-99i from the default you'll need to use the password change software for the EasyTouch-P to update it using your computer and a USB cable. It's a simple process, but it must be done with a PC. Perhaps a future firmware version will allow you to set the password in the settings screen to avoid having to hook the touch screen up to a computer.

The EasyTouch-P receives its power from the Ethernet jack, so you must use a Power-Over-Ethernet switch or a PoE Injector that complies with the IEEE 802.3af specification.

Configuring the EasyTouch-S

The software to configure the EasyTouch-S runs on your Windows computer. Mac or Linux users will need to use a virtual machine or borrow a computer to configure the device. Configuration can be a one-time only prospect if your system is well settled.

You configure your rooms, devices, scenes, and schedules using the software and simply download it into the touch screen via a USB cable. The USB port is easy to access even after the touchscreen has been permanently installed, so you can update the device without removing it.

Setting up devices was trivially easy, albeit a bit repetitive, and in less than thirty minutes I had the touch screen completely configured to control every device in my house. Setting up scenes is also trivially easy: Just add a new scene, name it, and drag and drop devices into the scene.

The desktop software has a few user interface quirks. While it is feature complete, additions such as toolbars, double-clicking to edit, would provide the finishing touches to make it more intuitive and easy to use. A feature to import devices, groups, and events from HouseLinc 2 would be a welcome addition.

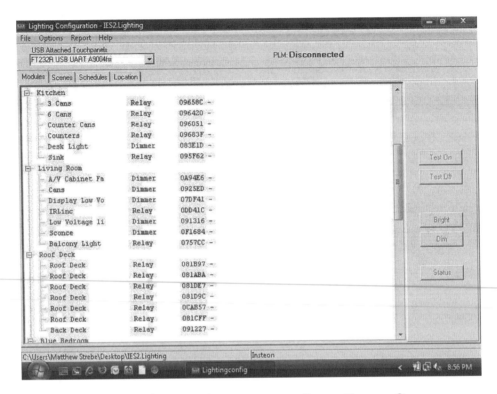

Figure 9.6: The touch screen configuration software

Discovering and troubleshooting using the PLM

The IES software can be used to directly control the PLM by connecting the PLM to your computer's serial port (via a USB to serial adapter if your computer lacks a serial port).

Directly controlling the PLM with the IES configuration software allows you to:

- Clear the existing PLM links if you are repurposing a PLM
- Discover devices by linking them to the PLM

- Test the functionality of INSTEON devices by directly controlling them

Modifying the look of the touch screen

IES provides software to completely redesign the screens in the EasyTouch devices. You can customize the icons, fonts, text, button placement, background, and screens to suit your needs or match your décor.

Figure 9.7: The screen design software

The software actually does more than IES supports. The software is included primarily for changing icons, changing backgrounds, and changing the text on the screens. Future versions may allow you to add buttons to screens and change the actions that buttons perform. While this software is more difficult to use than the room and device configuration software, its great for things like removing the IES logo or customizing the display with your family name.

You must disable your computer's "ClearType" feature in order to prevent Windows from modifying fonts that are downloaded to the device when you use the screen modification software. Instructions are provided with the device for Windows XP. Search Windows help on the term "ClearType" for instructions to disable it in Windows Vista or Windows 7. Even with ClearType disabled, most fonts don't look that great on the touch screen. You'll want to test buttons with many different fonts to find the ones that look best. Most fonts look best when they are bold and not italicized.

Installing the EasyTouch Tabletop Touchscreen

Tabletop versions of the touch screen are simple to deploy: Simply plug them in to a Category 5 cable and plug that cable either into your wired Ethernet port or your PLM plugged into an outlet.

Installing the EasyTouch in-wall Touchscreen

Installing the touchscreen in the wall is not difficult for anyone who is comfortable doing home repair. If you are not comfortable with these procedures or if you home does not lend itself to pulling new cable through the walls, purchase the tabletop versions of the EasyTouch instead.

Refer to the installation instructions that come with the IES EasyTouch before installing. The instructions in this book are provided to illustrate the installation procedure.

INSTALLING AN EASYTOUCH BY RUNNING CATEGORY 5 CABLE

⇒ Determine where you would like to install the EasyTouch touch screen. Using a fish tape, run a Category 5 cable to the location from your attic, and to either your Ethernet switch location (EasyTouch-P) or to a power outlet (EasyTouch-S). You may find it convenient to wire an outlet in your attic to accommodate a PLM for the EasyTouch-S.

⇒ Cut in and install a dual-gang junction box.

⇒ Terminate the Ethernet cable on both ends using RJ-45 jacks and a proper crimp tool. It may be easier to install a pre-terminated jumper cable if you can buy one long enough.

⇒ If you are using the EasyTouch-P, connect the terminated cable to your Ethernet switch. If your switch does not provide Power Over Ethernet, you will also need a PoE injector, which you can purchase from numerous sources online.

⇒ If you are using the EasyTouch-S, connect the terminated cable to your PLM an plug it in.

⇒ At the faceplate, plug the EasyTouch into the terminated cable and ensure that it powers up and operates correctly.

⇒ Screw the EasyTouch into the junction box and place the magnetic faceplate over it.

If you have wired Ethernet throughout your house, you can re-purpose an existing Ethernet outlet that is near the correct location.

INSTALLING AN EASYTOUCH-P IN PLACE OF AN EXISTING ETHERNET OUTLET

⇒ Remove the existing faceplate and remove the Ethernet Jack from it.

⇒ After determining that you will not be blocked by a stud, cut out and install a dual-gang junction box in the location where you would like to install the EasyTouch-P.

⇒ Using a fish-tape, pull a terminated Ethernet jumper between the location of the Ethernet jack and the location of the EasyTouch-P.

⇒ Plug the Ethernet Jack into the Ethernet Jumper and plate over the Ethernet outlet.

⇒ At your Ethernet switch location, connect the Ethernet cable going to the former Ethernet outlet to either a Power-over-Ethernet switch or a PoE power injector and regular switch.

⇒ Connect the EasyTouch-P to the Ethernet jumper. Ensure that it powers on correctly.

⇒ Screw the EasyTouch into the Junction Box being careful not to crimp any exposed wires, and place the magnetic faceplate cover over it.

If you're using the PLM version, the easiest way to install it will be directly next to or above an existing electrical outlet or switch.

INSTALLING AN EASYTOUCH-S WITHOUT RUNNING CABLE

⇒ Find a location directly next two or above an existing switch or outlet.

⇒ Open the existing switch or outlet and either remove the junction box or otherwise find a way to ensure that your location is easily reachable, that no studs block the path between your touchscreen location and the outlet or switch, and that at least 3" of space in the wall is available to accommodate the PLM and the touch screen.

⇒ Cut in and install a dual-gang junction box that does not have a back.

⇒ Cut off the outlet side of an extension cord and fish it through the wall to the switch that will provide power.

⇒ Wire the extension cord ground, LINE, and NEUTRAL wires to the existing switch or outlet using wirenuts.

⇒ At the new junction box cut in, plug your PLM into the extension cord and into a short Category 5 cable. Place the PLM inside the wall directly behind the junction box. Depending on available space, you may need to move the PLM around inside the wall.

⇒ Install the EasyTouch-S by screwing it into the dual-gang junction box. Place the magnetic faceplate on.

Using the EasyTouch

When you power on the EasyTouch, you'll be presented with a Welcome Screen. You'll see an IES logo and two or three buttons:

- Scenes
- Manual

- Schedules (EasyTouch-S only)

The IES logo is actually a secret setup button. By pressing and holding it, you'll enter a setup screen that will allow you to set the screen brightness and contrast, button beeps, and the time.

The Scenes button gives you access to the Scenes you setup. Up to six scenes will appear on screen, along with back, next, and home buttons. Pressing next and back will allow you to page among all of your scenes. Pressing home takes you back to the welcome screen.

On the EasyTouch-S, the Manual button brings up the Rooms button. Six rooms are shown per screen, and you can page between screens using back or next, with a home button to return to the main screen. When you click a room, you will see a button for every device configured in that room. The touch screen will immediately check the status of each device—if the device cannot be reached, the button will flash "no response," indicating the problem. A red dot appears in the corner whenever the Touch Screen is communicating over INSTEON. If the red dot stays too long, it may indicate a problem with the INSTEON network.

On the EasyTouch-P, the Manual button brings up the Home and Extra buttons. Extra allows you to directly access every one of your devices. However, there is no "Rooms" concept on the EasyTouch-P because there it receives its programming from the ISY-99i. To implement rooms, use the "Floor Plan" feature in the ISY-99i to group your devices, and the EasyTouch-P will then see those groupings. The EasyTouch-P does not have a schedules section because scheduled commands are handled by the ISY-99i.

Each button also has a level bar, and the currently selected device will have a green "LED" in the corner. When you select a device, you will see On and off buttons appear. If the device is a dimmer you will also see dim, brighten, and 25% and 50% buttons. Clicking these buttons controls the device as you would expect.

You can also press and hold the device button to toggle its state rather than pressing the on or off buttons. The red level lines will indicate the on/off or dim level of the device.

The EasyTouch-S also allows you to configure schedules for simple control of lights based on the time of day or based on dusk and dawn times for your location. The internal clock is battery backed in case of power failure. The EasyTouch-P does not incorporate scheduling because the ISY-99i performs those functions.

> Software and technical manuals for the EasyTouch touch screens are available at the IES website, which you can find in the Resources Appendix. You can download the software in advance of purchasing the unit to determine whether it will work for you.

If you want sophisticated touch screen functionality at your major points of entry, bedside table, or in your home theater, the IES EasyTouch devices are the best choice. They are the only touch screens designed specifically for INSTEON at the time of this writing, they're very easy to configure, and they do the job nicely.

Security System Integration

INSTEON has a number of options for integrating with security systems:

- Define a simple security system based entirely on INSTEON sensors and alarms, with no central alarm panel. This results in a medium cost, flexible, easily configured system but which lacks the capability of being centrally armed or disarmed. It's a simple stimulus-response system.
- Using the Elk M1 Gold INSTEON compatible alarm system. This is the most flexible and reliable, but also the most expensive and hardest to configure.
- Interfacing your existing typical alarm system to your INSTEON network using an INSTEON I/O controller. This is a low-cost

solution, but can probably only be used to trigger alarms and respond to them. It is easy to setup if you know how to program your existing alarm panel and are familiar with low voltage alarm wiring.

All three methods are detailed in this section.

Security integration with INSTEON devices

All security systems are relatively simple:

- Inputs are connected to simple sensors, such as magnetic closure sensors, switches, motion detectors, and temperature sensors.
- Controllers are programmed with rules to process inputs and determine when and which outputs to activate.
- Outputs are connected to alarms, such as bells, sirens, flashers, and actuators for fire suppression systems.

Sound familiar? Alarm panels are centralized stimulus-response systems. INSTEON is a de-centralized stimulus-response system, and fully capable of performing the same actions.

The web of links between INSTEON sensors and INSTEON responders replaces the central control panel of the typical alarm panels. Creating a simple and effective alarm system is as easy as linking sensors to responders connected to alarm devices.

As INSTEON technology has matured, new devices have come to the market that allow very simple integration of sensors that can be used to control INSTEON responders.

INSTEON Sensors

A wide range of INSTEON sensors are available that are trivially easy to install and configure. With a little more work, any traditional sensor can be connected to an alarm system through an I/O controller such as the INSTEON I/OLinc from SmartLabs or the EZIO line of devices from SimpleHomeNet.

- INSTEON motion sensors are particularly easy to use and quite small and reliable. They're also quite easy to program using HouseLinc.
- INSTEON Wireless open/close sensors can be placed anywhere in your home, without wires, and used to detect the opening of a door or window. You'll need an INSTEON Access Point in order to pick up the signal.
- INSTEON I/OLinc devices have one input and one output. They can be connected to a wide array of typical alarm sensors such as contact closures, water level sensors, or any other simple low voltage sensors, and can be used to control any single low voltage load. With numerous sensor modes and output latching states, INSTEON I/OLincs are an inexpensive, flexible, and easy to use. They are also easily configured via HouseLinc.
- EZSnsRF Dakota bridges have to be manually configured, but they can be immediately interfaced with wireless motion sensors, driveway sensors, and water level sensors.
- Any typical alarm system sensor can be integrated with INSTEON using an EZIO input device.
- Some EZIO devices also have Dallas Semiconductor 1-Wire interfaces that allow you to interface them with very inexpensive temperature and humidity sensors. A single 1-Wire interface can be connected to a number of sensors on a wire bus.

INSTEON Responders

SwitchLincs, ApplianceLincs, LampLincs, I/OLincs, and EZIO Output devices are all typical responders that can be used to indicate an alarm condition.

- ApplianceLincs can respond to any INSTEON device to activate a typical light or 120v bell or siren.
- I/O Link devices can be used to control a single low voltage device such as a typical alarm system bell or siren.

- EZIO devices have varying numbers of output of different types that can be used to control a wide array of low voltage devices.

With some minor additional electronic components (typically just a resistor) you can activate literally any electrical device with these components.

Ultimately what an INSTEON based alarm system will lack is the ability to make decisions when to alarm. For example, a true security system can be set to a disarmed state: Even if a security sensor was triggered, alarms will not go off. A true centralized security panel can process time of day filters and even complex logic. INSTEON can only achieve this level of complexity when combined with a home automation controller.

Elk M1 Gold Security System

The Elk M1 Gold Security System is a powerful and very flexible stand-alone security system. As such, it is a complex system in its own right. Using an Elk RS-232 adapter, a smarthome PLM, and a firmware upgrade, you can configure an Elk M1 Gold security system to send commands to INSTEON devices based on any security event or series of events.

> The ELK M1 Gold system can only control INSTEON devices. It cannot receive inputs from INSTEON devices over the INSTEON powerline network, but you can wire I/OLinc or EZIO devices to trigger the sensor inputs of the Elk System.

The biggest differentiator for the Elk M1 Gold system compared to most security systems (other than its INSTEON compatibility) is its powerful rule-based processing system. The Elk system can be configured to combine numerous sensors, time-of-day conditions, and other inputs to determine specific actions to take, such as activating alarms, sending INSTEON commands, dialing phone numbers, and so forth based on more than just a single input.

Consider why this is important: With INSTEON, a single motion sensor can trigger an alarm. But what if you only want that alarm to trigger ONLY when the motion sensor reports motion AND you have activated a light switch you use to indicate that you're home AND the time of day is between dusk and dawn? INSTEON alone can't do that because there's no one device to correlate all of those inputs to determine whether or not to trigger the output. The Elk M1 Gold can process its own security inputs (not INSTEON inputs) in complex ways to control INSTEON devices. The Elk system can also be dial-in controlled remotely when you are away.

While powerful, the Elk system is quite complex—easily as complex as an entire whole-home INSTEON system. I've installed alarm systems professionally early in my working days and I make my living as a computer systems integrator, and It took me two full days to get the system installed and operational all the way through to being able to send INSTEON commands.

I've found that the uses that I setup the Elk system to perform (such as turning on lights based on window closures detecting opening or motion sensors being triggered) are far easier and much less expensive to perform using INSTEON motion sensors, EZIO devices, or the EZSnsRF Dakota bridge. Programming the Elk system requires a computer, an Ethernet bridge or a direct serial connection to the panel, specialty software, and a rather steep learning curve. It doesn't come any where near the ease of use of INSTEON.

Ultimately, I would not consider installing an Elk M1 Gold system unless you wanted a full featured and independent security system anyway, you were doing it as part of a remodel or new construction, and you had professional installers do the heavy lifting for the initial programming (or you are at least as serious a geek as I am).

If you are just looking to detect a few sensors or to build a lightweight security system to retrofit in an existing home, I recommend rolling your own using INSTEON sensors and alarm lights or bells attached to appliance controllers.

Interfacing with traditional security systems

You may already have an existing security system that was not designed to be compatible with INSTEON systems. Although you may not be able to perform complex interactions such as enabling and disabling alarms, you will be able to use INSTEON devices to trigger alarms and respond to alarms.

All of these systems can be interfaced to an I/OLinc or EZIO I/O controller so long as they have at least one free input (if you want to activate or control the alarm) or one free output terminal (if you want to activate INSTEON devices when an alarm triggers).

To trigger an alarm or control your alarm panel, wire the output of an I/OLinc or EZIO device to an input terminal on your existing alarm system and link an INSTEON controller to the INSTEON I/O responder. For example, you could replace an existing Window Closure input with the output an I/OLinc, and when the I/OLink status became open, an alarm would sound.

To control INSTEON devices when an alarm triggers, wire the input of an I/OLinc or EZIO device to an output terminal on the existing alarm panel, and link the INSTEON I/O controller to the INSTEON responders you want to activate. For example you could replace an existing bell alarm with an the input of an I/OLink so that when an alarm was raised, the lights in your bedroom would come on rather than sounding a bell.

Directly wiring INSTEON I/O devices to alarm panel I/O terminals will typically require (at least) a resister wired in series, and you may have to configure the INSTEON I/O device for specific relay modes of operation. Check your alarm panel documentation for instructions regarding how to wire to simple contact closure inputs and outputs.

Interfacing alarm systems with INSTEON devices is relatively simple and straightforward for anyone with experience with low-voltage wiring systems. If you've never done work like this before, consider hiring an alarm system installer to help you out the first time you work with it.

Software for Home Computers

There are a large number of home automation programs and home automation controllers (which are really just special purpose computers that come pre-programmed with home automation software). Most home automation applications and controllers have at least some support for INSTEON—usually, they can be programmed to directly control lights when used with a PLM or PLC.

However, simply directly controlling lights does not provide INSTEON's most important feature: It's decentralized ability to remain operational even when devices and controllers fail thanks to the microcontroller built into every switch and the fact that links can be programmed into the devices themselves.

This is such an important feature that I decided to discuss only those programs which are capable not only of directly controlling INSTEON devices but also of managing the links programmed into INSTEON devices as well—creating, modifying, and deleting them as necessary and programming timed events into the PLM or PLC directly so that the computer and software need not be left running.

Indigo

Indigo is the premier home automation control program for Macintosh computers. It has evolved quickly since its introduction, gaining the ability to program links directly into devices and store events in the PLM so that the software need not be left running in order for your INSTEON scenes and events to work correctly.

If you have a Mac and do not have a PC, your only two low-cost options for managing INSTEON links are a Universal Devices ISY-99 or

Indigo. Both are good options, but Indigo is less expensive and more powerful—the only drawback is that your computer will be dedicated to managing your INSTEON network. Indigo requires an INSTEON USB PLC or an EZSrve or EZBridge from SimpleHomeNet.

mControl

mControl is a web-based control system that operates as three components: A windows PC or device-based web server, an editor program for Windows, and an Internet Explorer or Windows Media Center Edition specific web page. Like all web-page based user interfaces, there are delays and occasional glitches that you'll have to put up with. Normally, being based on a web page makes an application cross platform, but in the case of mControl, that's not the case—its web pages work only on Windows-based PCs. mControl connects through an INSTEON PLM.

Girder

Girder is a sophisticated home control application that targets more advanced users who want extremely sophisticated control over events and actions. The user interface is not intuitive by any means—you will have to read the instructions at a minimum.

Girder really targets those who are willing to perform some scripting in order to automate their home. For example, the standard Girder component, which costs $40, provides basic control of INSTEON devices. But because of Girder's extreme programmability, a motivated Girder user has created a far superior component that functions through a PLM and provides very detailed control of numerous INSTEON devices, as well as the ability to manage links in INSTEON devices—his component is free.

Girder can be thought of more as a platform for programmers to create components for end-users rather than a complete existing system in and of itself. Presuming that it attracts a large number of dedicated programmers, it has the potential to become the dominant home automation controller software for PCs.

Superna ControlWare

ControlWare provides a Windows Media Center-like interface for controlling your home from your PC or Windows CE-based PDA. Its primary focus is on direct control from your PC, rather than on home automation control as a dedicated server. It is relatively inexpensive.

Home Control Assistant

Home Control Assistant is a classic Windows application originally written to control X10 devices. Native INSTEON support was added in the 8th edition. HCA is a Windows application, so you must leave your computer turned on and logged in order to use it. It is capable of directly programming links into INSTEON devices from the scenes you create. HCA has a unique drag-and-drop event designer that allows you to create relatively sophisticated "flow-chart" style programs that can be triggered by a variety of events.

Summary

A wide and growing array of sophisticated devices and software applications can control INSTEON home automation devices, including low cost web controllers and software applications. You can use these tools to integrate all of your home systems while retaining INSTEON's strengths of reliability, fault tolerance, simplicity, and value.

Chapter 10
INSTEON Device Reference

INSTEON is a new and fast moving technology. There are dozens of devices available now and more coming all the time—no book could possibly hope to stay up to date. However, it is important for people considering INSTEON technology to have specific details of how INSTEON devices work and what they can do. It is also useful for determining which specific device or device category will fill a particular need.

This device reference is designed to show the range of options for the common best selling INSTEON devices at the time of this writing. As a snapshot of INSTEON technology, it should be considered an informative resource rather than an exhaustive catalog. Part numbers, prices, and availability will change rapidly, so be certain to search the Smarthome website for the current models at the time of your purchase.

This hardware matrix is organized by major category and then by specific devices within the category. I've included my personal opinions of these various devices when I own them and have used them in my personal installation. I've purchased all these devices myself unless otherwise noted, and my opinions of these devices when presented are mine alone. I also point out when I've not used a device in my network.

Phase Bridges

Every INSTEON installation requires a phase bridge. You have three options:

- For new construction or electrical remodels, use the SignaLinc Hardwired.
- For a reliable and easily installed hardwired solution when you aren't going to remodel, use the Plug-in 220V electrical dryer adapter.
- For apartments, homes without 220V service, or when you will use wireless INSTEON devices such as remote controls or motion sensors anyway, use the Access Points.

SignaLinc Hardwired

The SignaLinc Hardwired is a simple, reliable, and inexpensive device that an electrician can wire in next to your circuit breaker to provide permanent phase bridging in your home. Of all phase bridge options, the hardwired phase bridge is both the least expensive and most reliable, but it is also the most difficult to install. It needs to be connected at your main circuit panel across the two legs of your installation, so your panel will have to be wired for it.

SignaLinc 3-Wire or 4-Wire Plug-in Phase Bridge

The SignaLinc Plug-in Phase Bridge is an inexpensive, easily installed, and highly reliable device for bridging the phases in your home.

I recommend these plug-in phase bridges for any installation that has a compatible 220V outlet that is easily accessible—these phase bridges are more reliable than the RF INSTEON Access Points, which are subject to interference and distance limitations. Hard-wired solutions are always the most reliable, and the plug-in adapter is easily installed compared to the hardwired phase bridge.

Figure 10.1: SignaLinc Plug-in Phase Bridge

INSTEON Access Point

INSTEON Access Points act as wireless SignaLinc phase couplers and add the capability of repeating INSTEON signals from wireless INSTEON devices such as the RemoteLinc RF wireless handheld remote control, the INSTEON wireless motion sensor, and the INSTEON Wireless contact closure.

Access Points work well as phase couplers, but no wireless device can claim to be 100% reliable. If you use wireless phase couplers and find that you have problems controlling specific lights from distant switches, order a plug-in 220V phase coupler and see if that doesn't solve the problem. Your Access Points will still be useful as RF INSTEON repeaters for wireless INSTEON devices.

Access Points are very much Plug-and-forget devices—I haven't had a single problem with mine. I even have one plugged in outside in a very coastal region on our roof deck, and it has been operating just fine for a year inside a weatherproof electrical outlet cover. The operation of my RemoteLinc is reliable and has never missed a beat in over a year.

Prior to the release of the INSTEON access points, SmartLabs marketed a SignaLinc RF device that could only be used as a phase bridge. It is no longer sold, as Access Points are now available.

Figure 10.2: INSTEON Access Points

Switches and Dimmers

Switches and dimmers form the basis of an INSTEON smart home. They are either wired in or plugged in between lamps and dimmers and provide the ability to centrally control the lights to which they are attached. Timers provide the ability to automatically turn off lights after a certain period, and in some cases to turn them on based on the time of day.

SwitchLinc Relay and ToggleLinc Relay

SwitchLinc Relays are the basic INSTEON wired-in device. They replace light switches throughout your house with a switch that is computer controlled and can be linked to any other switch in your home. SwitchLinc Relays come with Decora-style paddle switches and have a line of LEDs along the left side of the paddle that show whether the switch is on or off.

SwitchLinc Relays are simple to install and are rated for loads up to 15 amps. The ToggleLinc Relay is the same electronically with a toggle-style switch.

	Relay	Dimmer	Timer
Decora	SwitchLinc Relay #2476S	SwitchLinc Dimmer #2476D	SwitchLinc Timer #2476ST
Toggle	ToggleLinc Relay #2466S	ToggleLinc Dimmer #2466D	NA
Keypad	KeypadLinc On/Off #2486S	KeypadLinc Dimmer #2486D	KeypadLinc Timer #2484D
Hidden	InLineLinc Relay #2475S	InLineLinc Dimmer #2475D	NA
2-Wire	2-Wire Switch #2474S	2-Wire Dimmer #2474D	NA
Plug-in Control	ApplianceLinc #2456S3	LampLinc #2456D3	TimerLinc #2456S3T
Outlet	OutletLinc Relay #2473S	NA	NA
Budget	ICON Relay #2856S3B	ICON Dimmer #2856D3B	NA
High Power	EZSwitch 30A relay #31278	SwitchLinc 1000 Dimmer#2476DH	NA

Table 10.2: INSTEON Switches and Dimmers

SwitchLinc Dimmer and ToggleLinc Dimmer

SwitchLinc Dimmers electronically switch the circuit to reduce the total amount of electricity flowing to the attached device. This will dim an incandescent light, low-voltage lights, and will slow magnetic loads such as fans.

The chopped power cannot be used to power appliances or incandescent lights because the interruption to power will cause the transformers in these devices to drop below the necessary power levels required to operate the devices. You should not install dimmers on fluorescent lights.

Dimmers also cause fans to vibrate and make a characteristic buzzing sound that may cause the device to wear out faster, so your mileage will vary if you attempt to use them to control fan speed. I've had good luck with this personally, but SmartLabs recommends driving fans with SwitchLinc Relays.

Figure 10.3: SwitchLinc Dimmer

Typical SwitchLinc dimmers are rated for 600-watt loads, but you should not go above 80% of the load rating when you design, which limits the devices to 500-watts. It is normal for dimmers to run warm to hot depending on how much power is being drawn through them.

When you need to control numerous lights from a single switch, use the 1000W-watt variant. The 1000W variant comes with a larger face heat sink that does not fit next to other devices in a multi-gang switchbox. You can break the heat sink ears off, but they reduce the rating of the switch by 100 watts for each of the four ears. If you remove two ears and place the switch next to anther switch in a multi-gang box, you've effectively de-rated the switch to 800 watts. Breaking off all four ears de-rates it to a typical 600-watt dimmer.

SwitchLinc dimmers can be set to come on at any reduced power rate, requiring the user to double-tap the on switch to come up to 100%. Setting lights to come on to 70% is a great way to save energy by default, and will keep multi-light fixtures from drawing enough power to generate a lot of heat in the switch.

Figure 10.4: ToggleLinc Relay

You can also configure SwitchLinc dimmers with a custom ramp-rate, which refers to the amount of time it takes for the light to come on. Slow ramp rates create dramatic lighting effects in front rooms and other show areas of the home. They also reduce the initial power surge that occurs when power comes on suddenly after an outage, and can help to prevent circuit breaker overload.

The ToggleLinc Dimmer is the same electronics with a toggle-style switch plate.

SwitchLinc Timer

The SwitchLinc Timer is a SwitchLinc Relay that has a built-in timer and can shut itself off after a programmable delay. You can set the delay manually using a complicated series of tap and set codes, or you can program the delay using HouseLinc. Use SwitchLinc Timers in rooms that are normally unoccupied such as bathrooms, closets, and utility rooms.

If you need easily changeable times for rooms such as bathrooms or garages where you may occasionally spend more time, consider the KeypadLinc Timer instead. It provides eight different pre-programmed delay time settings on the keypad.

There is no ToggleLinc version of the SwitchLinc Timer as of the time of this writing.

KeypadLinc On/Off

KeypadLinc On/Off is a SwitchLinc Relay with an additional set of backlit buttons that can be programmed to send commands to other devices. Each LED backlight can be controlled by the devices linked to a button to show whether the controlled device is on or off.

Figure 10.5: KeypadLinc 8-button Mode

KeypadLincs come in two varieties: 6-Button and 8-Button. Both are actually the same device with different faceplates, and you can convert them back and forth by simply swapping the faceplates.

In 6-button mode, the top ON and bottom OFF buttons control the local load in a manner that anyone can understand. The four central buttons are then used to control other INSTEON devices. 6-button KeypadLincs work great for replacing a single light switch with a keypad controller that won't confuse people who aren't aware of how your system works.

In 8-button mode, the A-button acts as a toggle for the local load, and the remaining seven buttons are available to be programmed to control other loads. Each button can be programmed to act as an ON only, OFF only, or toggle for any device or group of devices. The A-button will always control the local load, but you can install KeypadLincs without the load wire connected if you don't need to control a load. 8-button keypads are most appropriately used in multi-gang junction boxes where standard switches control the obvious lights and the KeypadLinc is used to control an auxiliary light.

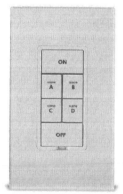

Figure 10.6: KeypadLinc in 6-button mode

The buttons can be used to control dimmable INSTEON devices even though the KeypadLinc is an on/off device. By holding the button down, DIM or Brighten commands are sent to bring lights up and down as you hold.

KeypadLinc Dimmer

The KeypadLinc Dimmer combines the features of the KeypadLinc On/Off with the dimmer electronics of the SwitchLinc Dimmer. All of the information regarding those two products applies to the KeypadLinc Dimmer.

KeypadLinc Timer

The KeypadLinc Timer is a version of the 8-button KeypadLinc that comes with a timer and the buttons engraved with eight different delay times from 2 minutes to 2 hours. The eight buttons are programmed to control the local load for different times, which makes the switch just a local load controller rather than a true "keypad"—you would not use the KeypadLinc Timer to control multiple loads.

The KeypadLinc timer is especially convenient for bathrooms and garages where people spend widely differing amounts of time.

Figure 10.7: KeypadLinc Timer

InLineLinc Relay

The InLineLinc Relay is a SwitchLinc Relay without the front switch. It is designed to be controlled by other INSTEON devices, and can be hidden in walls or ceilings behind other fixtures. You can use InLineLinc Relays to convert a large gang of switches to be controlled by a RemoteLinc or a KeypadLinc, for example, or to convert fixtures in the ceiling to be controllable separately from other fixtures when they had originally been wired to come up together.

InLineLinc Dimmer

The InLineLinc Dimmer is an InLineLinc Relay with the same dimmer electronics as a SwitchLinc Dimmer.

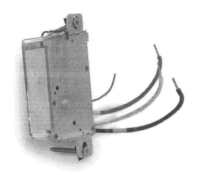

Figure 10.8: InLineLinc Relay

2-Wire Switch

The INSTEON 2-Wire Switch is an ICON Relay switch with the faceplate made separate from the Relay controller. This allows you to install the relay controller at the fixture and convert the switch-leg traveler from HOT + LOAD to HOT + NEUTRAL, which provides the Neutral necessary for INSTEON devices. It's a clever solution to the Neutrals problem. The switch faceplate and relay controller have the same INSTEON ID and cannot be used separately from one another.

2-Wire Dimmer

The INSTEON 2-Wire Dimmer is the same thing as the INSTEON 2-Wire switch, but with Dimmer electronics rather than a relay.

ApplianceLinc

The ApplianceLinc is one of the core INSTEON devices. It is a plug-in INSTEON responder that provides a relay controlled switched outlet that you can plug any home appliance into.

Figure 10.9: ApplianceLinc

LampLinc

The LampLinc is the same thing as an ApplianceLinc with Dimmer electronics. It should only be used to control incandescent lamps.

TimerLinc

The TimerLinc is similar to an ApplianceLinc but it has no pass-through outlet and instead provides an LCD showing the time and a set of buttons that can be used to manually configure the timer. ApplianceLinc Timers can control themselves and any number of other INSTEON devices, but they have only a single set of timers—all connected devices receive the on/off commands as a set, including the timer itself. You can program up to fourteen different on/off commands throughout the day or week. TimerLincs are especially convenient for controlling holiday lighting.

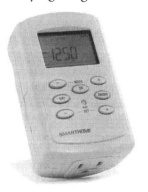

Figure 10.10: TimerLinc

Figure 10.11: OutletLinc Relay

OutletLinc Relay

The OutletLinc Relay is an ApplianceLinc in the form-factor of a typical Two-Outlet socket. It has one controlled outlet and one pass-through outlet. There is no dimmer version available because there's no way to be certain that the loads that will be plugged in are incandescent dimmable loads.

ICON Relay

The ICON Relay is a low cost version of the SwitchLinc Relay. It uses a mechanical relay rather than an electronic one, and it has a single low-cost amber LED rather than a row of white LEDs. Otherwise they are functionally the same.

ICON Dimmer

The ICON Dimmer is a lower cost version of the SwitchLinc Dimmer. It uses lower cost electronics and has a single amber LED rather than a row of white LEDs and does not show the approximate dim level. Otherwise they are functionally the same.

Figure 10.12: EZSwitch30 Relay

EZSwitch 30 30A relay

The EZSwitch 30 relay is similar to an ApplianceLinc but it comes with a high-amperage relay for loads that are too high to switch with an ApplianceLinc. In addition to handling high-amperage 120V loads, it is also capable of switching 220V loads such as HVAC compressors, pool pumps, etc. the EZSwitch 30 must be wired into the circuit using screw-post terminals.

Technology Bridges

Technology Bridges adapt INSTEON to other technologies, such as television remotes, the Internet, and other wired and wireless systems. The functionality provided varies widely depending on the technology being adapted.

Technology	Device
INSTEON-RF	Access Point #2443
Dakota Wireless Sensors	EZSnsRF #31275
IR for television remotes	IRLinc #2411R, EZUIRT #31281, ISY-99/IR #12232P
X-10 RF	EZX-10RF #31276
Ethernet	EZSrve #31279
USB	Powerline Modem #2412UH
Serial	Powerline Modem #2412S
Internet	EZSrve #31279, SmartLinc #2412N, ISY-99 #12231

Table 10.3: INSTEON Technology Bridges

Powerline Modem

INSTEON Powerline modems allow devices like computers, home automation controllers, and keypad interfaces to communicate with INSTEON devices. They are required for a broad range of computers and controller devices.

Powerline modems are simple devices that connect via RS-232 serial ports and simply interpret ASCII strings representing INSTEON commands to be transmitted on the wire, and a few simple commands to manage the link table and (in some models) a timer table. There are slightly different models, so be sure to purchase the model specified by your computer software or home automation controller.

Powerline Controller

Powerline Controllers are Powerline modems with a timer, a simple microcontroller, and additional memory built-in, which allows them to perform simple event processing and allows them to execute simple programs written in the SmartLabs "Salad" programming language. Because reliability problems with Powerline Controllers have not been resolved and because they require the installation of a software device manager on the host computer, SmartLabs is phasing them out in favor of the simpler and more universally supported Powerline Modem.

EZSnsRF

The EZSnsRF bridges Dakota compatible wireless security sensors with INSTEON, allowing the Dakota line of long-range motion detectors, fluid level sensors, driveway pressure sensors and contact closures to trigger INSTEON events.

Linking devices with an EZSnsRF is an easy but manual process that is very specific—you'll want to have a set of instructions with you each time you perform the operation.

From the factory, the EZSnsRF sends an ON command when the sensor triggers, and an OFF command when the sensor is finished triggering. This is usually about 30 seconds for a motion sensor, which will cause a light to come on only momentarily. You can change the delay up to 15 minutes, but no longer. The EZSnsRF is designed more for security alerting than for convenience lighting. If you need a longer delay, look to the INSTEON Wireless motion sensors.

EZX-10RF

The EZX-10RF allows X10 remote controllers (including HomeLinc integrated garage door openers) to trigger INSTEON events. It also acts as an X10 to INSTEON repeater, allowing you to use the entire range of inexpensive X10 sensors with a reliable INSTEON signal (rather than hoping the X10 signal reaches INSTEON devices that you would like to control).

Figure 10.13: EZSrve Web Controller

EZSrve

The EZSrve is a low-cost web interface for INSTEON and X10 networks that can be used with most web browsers to provide web-based control of your INSTEON system. It is mid-way between the SmartLinc and the ISY-99 in terms of functionality, upgradability, and cost. Its primary features are its strong scene and event management features and the fact that it does not require an external PLM.

SmartLinc

The SmartLinc is a simple, low-cost web interface to your INSTEON system specifically designed to turn your Apple iPhone or iPod Touch into a remote control over existing wireless computer network. It is fast, functional, works well, and costs only $120 at the time of this writing.

ISY-99

The ISY-99 is a fully-fledged home automation controller for less than $400 (plus the cost of a PLM). It can program links in all of your INSTEON devices, and can perform the functions of a SmartLinc, the HouseLinc software package, and an IRLinc (some models). It is completely cross-platform, running on Windows, Macintosh, and Linux, and can be controlled by a range of home automation technologies such as Windows Media Center, The Nokia 800 Web pad, and the Elk M1 Gold security and alarm panel. Chapter 9 details the ISY-99i fully.

Figure 10.14: ISY-99i Home Automation Controller

I/O Controllers

I/O controllers provide a standard way to adapt a large number of existing sensors such as contact closures and flood sensors to INSTEON and allow you to control low voltage devices such as security panels, door locks, sprinklers, HVAC, and most other home systems to control and be controlled by your INSTEON system.

Device	Out	In	Notes	Purpose
I/OLinc #2450	1	1	30VDC@5A max	Sensor, trigger
EZIO2x4 #31274	2	4	Ratings same as EZIO4O & EZIO6I	General purpose
EZIO4O #31283	4	0	30VDC or 120VAC 0.5A	Small loads <0.5A
EZIO6I #31280	0	6	4 0-30VDC, 2 0-5VDC	Sensors
EZIO8T	8	3	Low-VAC loads only; 1-wire input	Sprinkler, HVAC, Temp
EZIO8SA #31273P	8	7	Requires PLM; 1-wire input;	Loads < 3A, sensors, Temp
EZFlora #31270	8	0	24VAC Sprinkler valves & pump	Irrigation w/timer

Figure 10.4: INSTEON I/O Controllers

I/OLinc

I/OLinc allows you to monitor and control alarm sensors and triggers such as contact closures, garage-door sensors, door strikes, bells, and other low-voltage devices. The I/OLinc has one input and one output, and can be programmed for different modes of operation to match the attached devices.

Figure 10.15: I/O Linc

EZIO Series

SimpleHomeNet makes the widest array of INSTEON compatible I/O controllers. EZIO devices are significantly more programmable than the low cost I/OLinc devices and include a wide range of triggering, timing, and configuration options to allow the control and monitoring of a very broad range of devices such as alarm sensors, temperature sensors, and low-voltage DC or AC loads.

- The EZIO2x4 provides two isolated inputs, two analog level inputs, and two low-voltage I/O outlets
- The EZIO40 provides four outputs similar to the EZIO2x4.
- The EZIO6I provides six inputs similar to the EZIO2x4.
- The EZIO8T provides 3 digital inputs (including one 1Wire input for temperature and environment sensors) and 8 0-48VAC triac controlled outputs. The EZIO8T is specifically designed for controlling small AC loads such as sprinkler valves, model railroads, and HVAC dampers.
- The EZIO8SA is a large general purpose I/O controller with 4 opto-isolated general purpose sensors for alarm-type inputs, two 0-5V

line-level analog inputs for environmental sensors, and a 1-Wire bus input compatible with Dallas Semiconductors environmental sensors. It also has eight general-purpose 3A output relays rated for 120VAC or 30VDC loads. The EZIO8SA requires a PLM to interface to INSTEON networks.

Figure 10.16: EZIO 2x4 I/O Controller

EZFlora

The EZFlora irrigation controller is an I/O controller specifically designed to drive eight 24VAC sprinkler valves. It includes a heavy-duty 24VAC transformer to operate sprinkler valves, and has sophisticated timers built-in. A computer is required to configure the EZFlora timers, but not required to remain on to operate the sprinkler valves. EZFlora is supported by most common INSTEON home automation software packages.

Controllers

Controllers are devices that make it convenient to control INSTEON lighting and appliances in a variety of situations.

Controllers should be purchased only after you have your INSTEON system installed and working with standard devices such as SwitchLincs and

KeypadLincs. Once you've identified a specific control need for your system, purchase the device that will handle that specific need. Buying controllers based on their features rather than your requirements will cause you to waste money on devices that you find you don't actually use.

Figure 10.17: RemoteLinc

Of the myriad of control options we have for controlling lights in our house, including the Elk security system, IRLinc, EZSrve, SmartLinc, ISY-99, RemoteLinc, and HouseLinc, the only one we routinely use is well-configured KeypadLincs by the doors. They work the way light switches are supposed to work, and they're simple enough for everyone to understand. Nobody in the home except me uses the complex controllers with menus and screens because they're simply not intuitive, and because the KeypadLincs do the job really well.

RemoteLinc

The RemoteLinc wireless hand-held remote control provides a convenient way to control up to six different INSTEON devices or scenes from anywhere in your home.

I have a RemoteLinc, and to be frank I rarely use it. The only thing we actually use it for is controlling our exterior lighting when we're out on the deck. Inside the home, placing KeypadLinc controllers in high-traffic areas is a more convenient and natural way to control lighting than using a remote control, because the remote control is simply never around when you need it. Another convenient option if you already have an iPhone that you carry with you is to incorporate the SmartLinc controller on your wireless network. With an iPhone, the remote is always on your person.

When you're programming a home automation controller or software application, be aware that INSTEON Wireless devices such as the RemoteLinc cannot be discovered by HouseLinc Software or other INSTEON control solutions that "crawl" the network because they go into standby mode a few minutes after being used. In order to discover or link control software to them, you must wake the remote up by controlling a device with it immediately prior to linking or modifying links.

The RemoteLinc requires at least one INSTEON Access Point, and may require more depending upon the size of your home.

Figure 10.18: IRLinc

IRLinc

The IRLinc allows you program the universal remote control for your A/V system to control lights. By placing the IR receiver near your television you can assign various remote codes to INSTEON links.

I'm quite disappointed in the IRLinc. It is very difficult to program—you basically have to learn every remote code and then link each INSTEON device manually, and there is no easy way to change or recode the device other than to factory reset it and start over. Even using HouseLinc doesn't help—In HouseLinc, you see 50 arbitrarily numbered Group Codes with no good way to determine which remote code they actually represent other than to remember the order you learned the IR codes in and hope that they all registered correctly.

SmartHome needs to create a mode of operation with pre-programmed button codes from a well-supported remote, so that you can use HouseLinc to create a link to (for example) the "Play" button rather than requiring remote code learning. Until they've done that, I can't recommend the IRLinc. Once they do it, it'll be a fantastic device.

EZUIRT

The EZUIRT is an IR receiver and re-transmitter that will allow you to use your universal remote to control INSTEON devices, and to repeat INSTEON signals to IR components in your A/V cabinet. The EZUIRT can control devices using up to eight remote wired IR emitters, similar to an "IR Blaster."

I don't have an EZUIRT and can't write about how well it works. I use a Harmony 890 RF remote to control my A/V devices in my cabinet and an IRLinc to bridge IR to INSTEON.

ControlLinc

The ControlLinc is an inexpensive plug-in tabletop controller that provides five on/off button pairs and a set of buttons for controlling all of your devices.

As an inexpensive plug-in controller, the ControlLinc is ideal for situations where you cannot use wired-in devices. It works perfectly well with plug-in ApplianceLincs and LampLincs to provide INSTEON control for rented homes and apartments or in temporary situations. That said, it is quite large and not particularly attractive.

If you're just "getting your feed wet" with INSTEON while you evaluate whether or not to install a whole-home system, get a KeypadLinc Tabletop controller instead. You won't continue using the ControlLinc for long once you've installed a whole home system. The KeypadLinc Tabletop can be re-wired to become an in-wall KeypadLinc, so you won't have wasted a device. After initially testing INSTEON technology, I gave away my ControlLinc to a friend who was just getting started with INSTEON.

Figure 10.19: KeypadLinc Tabletop

KeypadLinc Tabletop

The KeypadLinc tabletop controller is simply a KeypadLinc wired to a cord and placed inside a plastic enclosure that angles it for easy use on a table. It's actually a really good idea—it's both more functional and more attractive than the ControlLinc, and can be re-wired as a wall switch if you should ever decide you no longer need a tabletop controller.

IES EasyTouch Touchscreen LCD

The EasyTouch allows you to control INSTEON scenes and devices using an intuitive and flexible touchscreen interface. The touch screens come in two models: A PLM version and a Power-over-Ethernet version.

Figure 10.20: IES EasyTouch LCD

Scenes and devices are programmed into the EasyTouch-S using your computer. It must be connected to an INSTEON 2412S PLM, which provides power and an INSTEON interface. In the case of an in-wall unit, this means that you'll have to run a serial cable through the wall to the PLM, which would have to be plugged in unobtrusively. There is not enough room left in the junction box to accommodate the PLM, so professional installation should be considered.

The EasyTouch-P is wired to your home Ethernet network and communicates via an ISY-99i that you must have installed. You do not program this version as it downloads scenes and devices directly from the ISY-99i.

The IES EasyTouch Touchscreen Color LCD controller comes in two versions: An in-wall unit that can be mounted inside a double-gang wall box, and a tabletop unit that comes in a plastic enclosure.

INSTEON Motion Sensor

The INSTEON Motion Sensor allows simple light activation by motion for lights in your home. It is an indoor unit—for outdoor needs, use the EZSnsRF Dakota with Dakota outdoor motion sensors.

The motion sensor is very easy to use—simply press the set button on it and link it to the lights you want to control. The motion sensor includes a timer that will turn the light back off after a set period of time.

Figure 10.21: INSTEON Motion Sensor

There is one substantial problem with the motion sensor: If you have the light on and the motion sensor activates, it will send an on command that will be ignored. But it will also send an off command when the timer expires, which means that a light you'd intended to have on will go off unexpectedly a few minutes after someone walks by the motion sensor.

The proper mode of operation would be for the motion sensor to first determine whether the light is on or off, and avoid sending an off command if the light is already on. This would introduce a delay in turning on the light, unfortunately.

Elk M1 Gold

The Elk M1 Gold security alarm panel is a full-feature alarm control system. It is quite flexible and complex, and can be used to control INSTEON devices from the alarm system keypads. The complete system required to connect the Elk to your INSTEON system and interface it with your computer system for programming will run to about $1000, so you need to be certain that its going to meet your needs.

I have the Elk system in my home and have configured it completely for use, but we don't use it to control lights. It's far simpler to control lights with a KeypadLinc than it is to look at the Elk keypad, scroll through the user interface, and select the device that you want to control.

This is actually a basic problem with all complicated control interfaces—having a menu system that you have to focus on requires far more mental effort than flipping a switch or pushing a button.

Summary

A broad range of INSTEON devices are available to complete your lighting, environment, security, and home entertainment smarthome. Check the Smarthome website periodically to see what new devices are available, but be led by your requirements rather than the possibilities if you want to build a truly useful system.

Chapter 11
Conclusion

It's been a year since we moved into our INSTEON SmartHome, and I've been very impressed withe the reliability and functionality of the system. We use the basic functionality of scene lighting, path lighting, and multi-way switching all the time.

More complex scenarios, such as those involving automated time-of-day switching, motion detection, or I/O-based switching are far less common in our home. We have just a few of those devices in constant use, mostly in the garage. We have one INSTEON motion sensor in the house that turns on a light in the living room if someone moves through the house in the dark.

Mistakes I've made

I broke the heat-sink tabs off of my first 1000w SwitchLinc Dimmer without realizing that they were required, and sure enough, it overheated driving our 720 watt chandelier after six months and locked up. SmartHome kindly replaced it, and informed me of the reason for the mistake.

I tried to use both HouseLinc and an ISY-99i at the same time on the same network. They tended to "fight" one-another over the link tables in devices, but they work together better than either manufacturer designed them to. In any case, you should pick one or the other and not try to use both. I prefer HouseLinc, but I think most people would prefer the ISY-99i.

Constantly reprogramming your devices is a recipe for convincing your spouse not to use the system. There will certainly be a settling period, but I've learned to get my wife's input on changes I'm planning to make prior to making them, just as I'd expect if she were going to repaint a room.

I tried to drive an EZSnsRF from a square-wave inverter instead of home power. It never worked again. Don't try this.

Components that have failed

Aside from the 1000w Dimmer that I broke, we haven't had a device actually fail.

We have had two devices "lock up" and require a manual reset, however:
- A KeypadLinc Dimmer seems to have lost its state requiring a manual reset after having been modified by an ISY-99i while HouseLinc was also active on the network. This was caused by my testing for this book, and is unlikely to happen to you.
- A KeypadLinc timer seemed to fail. One day, without apparent reason, it simply no longer worked and did not control it's load. I performed a factory reset, and it came back to life as if nothing had happened. This is the one and only issue we've had that I didn't directly cause, and it has not reoccurred.

That's it for problems we've had with the fifty-odd INSTEON devices we have installed around the house. Reliability has been on par with any other electrical device in my experience.

Components I've purchased but don't really use

The biggest cost in my network that I haven't spent the time to really integrate well is the Elk-M1 Gold. For me, security systems are simply annoying. I forget that I've set them and they go off. I suppose I just don't really care about security. I did all the work to get the ELK working and integrated with INSTEON, and then realized that there weren't any lights that I needed to turn on if a window opened. I was also disappointed by the fact that the ELK could control INSTEON devices, but not vice-versa. I may eventually do the integration work, but I need an INSTEON indicator of some sort that is more "alarm like" than turning on lights, without being annoying.

My wife uses the IES Touchscreen, but I usually don't. She likes the fact that the touch-screen "walks you through" the system, whereas I basically know what's going to happen with a particular button because I programmed the system. To be honest, she is reluctant to learn the KeypadLinc button functions because I keep changing them.

I purchased an IRLinc with high hopes, but the difficulty in programming it combined with a lack of support for it in HouseLinc at the time of this writing simply makes it too much trouble for me to bother with for anything beyond turning the A/V fans on and off. SmartHome needs to establish a fixed set of codes for the device and name them out of the box, so that I can choose the "Pause" button group and assign commands to it, rather than having to program the groups with IR codes first. The codes could then be cleared by someone who has to make them match a different universal remote if necessary.

I setup an EZSnsRF with outdoor motion sensors to turn on lights if it detected movement, but it turns out that it mostly picks up myself and my father-in-law coming home after dark, and winds up being an annoyance to people in the house. After slowly removing all the lights that are turned on by it, I relegated it to the garage, where the motion sensors turn the lights on and off when we come and go. It works well there, but INSTEON motion sensors would have been cheaper.

Between the ISY-99i, the EZSrve, and the SmartLinc, I use the SmartLinc most often, primarily because I have an iPhone and the user interface was designed for it. The ISY-99i is the best all-around solution, and the EZSrve has a lot of potential, but because I've chosen to go with HouseLinc for automated programming and I already have an iPhone, the SmartLinc works best for me. I used the EZSrve a lot more before I got the SmartLinc. My major annoyance with the SmartLinc is how badly its clock drifts. Smarthome seriously needs to support the Internet Network Time Protocol to make timed events more useful on the SmartLinc.

I have four OutletLincs that I've never installed. The portability of the ApplianceLincs works far better for me. I'm considering installing an OutletLinc on my Cablemodem to remotely reset it.

I purchased an EZIO8SA with grand plans to automate the gas fireplace switching, but have yet to do that. There's no easy place to hide the necessary PLM and the EZIO8SA itself. I find I use the INSTEON I/OLincs more often because I generally only have one I/O problem at any given location, so the EZIO devices can be overkill.

Summary

The core of my experience is that I tend to use the basic INSTEON devices and functionality heavily, but with rare exception, the more complex devices are rarely used. I strongly recommend putting off the purchase of complex devices until you know you have a need for them.

I use KeypadLincs at every major entryway and high-traffic area as our primary controllers for the system. We rarely use remote controls, web controllers, or touchscreens to control anything. KeypadLincs are more accessible to guests who have no knowledge of how the system works as well. It's likely that they will be your primary controllers as well.

I initially only purchased switches for the lights we knew we wanted to automate. I've since gone back through and replaced nearly every manual switch in the house with an INSTEON switch. If you're building new construction, save yourself the bother and spec every wired-in switch as an INSTEON switch.

Be prepared to move even some wired-in switches around. I've got a few relays controlling dimmable lights that I still need to swap out, and many of my KeypadLincs have moved from their original locations. You can't expect to figure out every possible use case in advance.

Good Luck!

Resources

www.insteon.net

The resource website for INSTEON development partners, alliance partners, and press. This site contains new press releases and technology information about the INSTEON protocol.

www.smarthome.com

Smarthome.com is the primary ecommerce website for SmartLabs, the developers of INSTEON technology, and as such it sells nearly all INSTEON related hardware and software.

www.simplehomenet.com

SimpleHomeNet developed the next-highest number of INSTEON devices after SmartLabs, and was first to market with a web controller and with I/O devices. SimpleHomeNet has the widest assortment of I/O controllers for INSTEON in their EZIO line, and has the broadest range of INSTEON enabled environment controllers. Their EZSrve and EZBridge devices are required by a number of home automation controllers and software applications for INSTEON control.

s.com

...er of the ISY-99, which is the most important
... INSTEON as of this writing.

...m

... subset of equipment and software for
...cintosh compatible—which is to say all INSTEON
...ces, and Mac compatible software. They primarily focus on Indigo for
software control.

www.perceptiveautomation.com

Perceptive Automation develops and markets Indigo home control software
for Apple Macintosh computers. With version 4, it is the most advanced
INSTEON home control software for the Macintosh market, and superior
to most PC based solutions.

www.promixis.com

Proximis develops the Girder home control platform, which is home
automation software that focuses on being highly extensible. It allows for
the relatively easy development of plug-in modules to control equipment,
allowing its user community to support one another by trading their
scripts.

www.powerhome.com

Power Home is a classic X10 home control application that has been updated
to include INSTEON support.

www.linuxha.com

Linux Home Automation is the blog site of the author of "Linux Smarthomes
for Dummies." While only peripherally involved in INSTEON, the site links
to the most comprehensive selection of Linux home control software that
is INSTEON compatible. Most Linux INSTEON development has stalled
because of the availability of the low cost and Linux compatible ISY-99.

www.elkproducts.com

Elk Products marks the Elk M1 security alarm panel, which has been moving into the home automation market through successive firmware updates. Now Linux compatible with the addition of an RS-232 interface and an INSTEON PLM, the Elk M1 system provides lighting and security integration.

www.wintrol.com

Wintrol makes and markets casement window closures motors that allow you to add automated control of windows to your scenes. While not specifically developed for INSTEON, they can easily be controlled by INSTEON I/O devices.

www.cortexa.com

Cortexa makes a line of home automation controllers and touch-screen interfaces capable of controlling INSTEON devices.

www.eyeonautomation.com

EYEON Automation makes a home automation controller that is compatible with INSTEON.

www.garagehawk.com

Garage Hawk is an INSTEON compatible garage door closer that can be remotely operated to ensure that you never leave your garage door open again.

www.iescorp-usa.com

IES make a line of touch screens that are INSTEON compatible. Using your PC, you can program the devices you'd like to be able to control and upload the settings into the touchscreen via USB.

Index

Made in the USA